Neil Kaminsky, LCSW

Man Talk
The Gay Couple's Communication Guide

Pre-publication
REVIEWS,
COMMENTARIES,
EVALUATIONS . . .

"**N**eil Kaminsky has humbly, wisely, and experientially tackled an important, often unexplored, area of gay men's relationships and intimacy. His writing is accessible, stimulating, and practical. When he explores complex issues such as male communication, couple dynamics, passive-aggressive behavior, interracial issues, he approaches the explanation of theory in a common-sense, clear, comprehensive, and witty manner.

As a therapist in private practice, I would refer to Kaminsky's guide myself for ideas, especially the great chapters on sex, anger, and 'The Seven Taboo Topics.' I would be excited to refer my individual gay male clients and gay couples to this book for challenge, inspiration, and a clearer understanding of their situation and choices."

Thomas J. Caldarola, MA, MDiv, MFT
Psychotherapist in private practice

"**N**eil Kaminsky has done it again! Combining vast clinical experience, good common sense, and unexpected wry humor, he shows us in this, the third in his trilogy of books on gay male relationships, how to negotiate the ambivalence, the confusion, and the contradictions inherent in human connection. Simply written, free of technical jargon, Kaminsky goes directly to the heart of those central dilemmas that confront couples in their quest to remain together or, in some cases, who choose to separate and move on. Particularly insightful are the sections on better managing anger and developing greater cultural sensitivity, both of which can either make or break a budding relationship or a long-term one. Suggested exercises, for either one partner or both, only serve to enhance the usefulness of this text, one that I would highly recommend to those gay men—in therapy or not—as well as to those of us therapists who struggle hard to help."

Andrew R. Gottlieb, PhD
Author, *Out of the Twilight:*
Fathers of Gay Men Speak;
Editor, *Interventions with Families of Gay,*
Lesbian, Bisexual, and Transgender People:
From the Inside Out

More pre-publication
REVIEWS, COMMENTARIES, EVALUATIONS . . .

"Neil Kaminsky recognizes the amount of work and energy required to maintain a positive relationship. This guide should reaffirm your good communication habits, challenge you to reconsider your less-positive communication actions, and better understand those of your partner. Drawing upon his years of experience as a therapist, Kaminsky guides us through the sometimes mystifying world of interpersonal communication by pointing out sound communication practices. These practices are made clear with his use of quotes from interviews and hypothetical vignettes."

Rick C. Roberts, MA
Department of Communication Studies,
University of San Francisco

"Kaminsky's common sense, comprehensive, and good-humored advice for gay couples is invaluable. I'm going to make it required reading for everyone I work with in counseling."

Robert H. Hopcke, MFT
Author, *Jung, Jungians and Homosexuality*

"Neil Kaminsky utilizes straightforward language and concrete examples to make complex psychological issues more understandable to the general reader. He uses a nonjudgmental approach to common emotional issues while providing tools to understand ourselves better and try to improve our capacity to relate to others, whether in a gay, intimate relationship or even in platonic friendships. Mr. Kaminsky addresses difficult issues such as sexuality and cultural norms in a very open fashion that allows the reader to feel comfortable with societal taboos. He is also careful to define the limits of the book and refers the reader to more specialized treatment when needed. *Man Talk* is easy to read and very informative. It is a good resource for any therapist working with relationship issues in the lesbian, bisexual, gay, and transsexual community."

Adelardo M. Ferrer, MD
General and child psychiatrist
in private practice; Child psychiatrist,
ACCESS Team, San Mateo County
Mental Health Services, San Mateo, CA

HPP
Harrington Park Press®
The Trade Division of The Haworth Press, Inc.
New York • London

NOTES FOR PROFESSIONAL LIBRARIANS AND LIBRARY USERS

This is an original book title published by Harrington Park Press®, The Trade Division of The Haworth Press, Inc. Unless otherwise noted in specific chapters with attribution, materials in this book have not been previously published elsewhere in any format or language.

CONSERVATION AND PRESERVATION NOTES

All books published by The Haworth Press, Inc., and its imprints are printed on certified pH neutral, acid-free book grade paper. This paper meets the minimum requirements of American National Standard for Information Sciences-Permanence of Paper for Printed Material, ANSI Z39.48-1984.

DIGITAL OBJECT IDENTIFIER (DOI) LINKING

The Haworth Press is participating in reference linking for elements of our original books. (For more information on reference linking initiatives, please consult the CrossRef Web site at www.crossref.org.) When citing an element of this book such as a chapter, include the element's Digital Object Identifier (DOI) as the last item of the reference. A Digital Object Identifier is a persistent, authoritative, and unique identifier that a publisher assigns to each element of a book. Because of its persistence, DOIs will enable The Haworth Press and other publishers to link to the element referenced, and the link will not break over time. This will be a great resource in scholarly research.

Man Talk
The Gay Couple's Communication Guide

Man Talk
The Gay Couple's Communication Guide

Neil Kaminsky, LCSW

HPP

Harrington Park Press®
The Trade Division of The Haworth Press, Inc.
New York • London

For more information on this book or to order, visit
http://www.haworthpress.com/store/product.asp?sku=5527

or call 1-800-HAWORTH (800-429-6784) in the United States and Canada
or (607) 722-5857 outside the United States and Canada

or contact orders@HaworthPress.com

Published by

Harrington Park Press®, the trade division of The Haworth Press, Inc., 10 Alice Street,
Binghamton, NY 13904-1580.

PUBLISHER'S NOTE
The development, preparation, and publication of this work has been undertaken with great care.
However, the Publisher, employees, editors, and agents of The Haworth Press are not responsible
for any errors contained herein or for consequences that may ensue from use of materials or information contained in this work. The Haworth Press is committed to the dissemination of ideas and information according to the highest standards of intellectual freedom and the free exchange of ideas.
Statements made and opinions expressed in this publication do not necessarily reflect the views of
the Publisher, Directors, management, or staff of The Haworth Press, Inc., or an endorsement by
them.

Cover design by Kerry E. Mack.
TR: 5.08.07; 5.22.07

Library of Congress Cataloging-in-Publication Data

Kaminsky, Neil, 1951-
    Man talk : the gay couple's communication guide / Neil Kaminsky.
        p. cm.
    Includes bibliographical references and index.
    ISBN: 978-1-56023-569-9 (hard : alk. paper)
    ISBN: 978-1-56023-570-5 (soft : alk. paper)
1. Gay couples. 2. Interpersonal communication. I. Title.

    HQ76.K318 2007
    646.7'8086642—dc22

                                                                        2006035432

For Virgilio

ABOUT THE AUTHOR

Neil Kaminsky, LCSW, is the author of *Affirmative Gay Relationships: Key Steps in Finding a Life Partner* (Haworth) and *When It's Time to Leave Your Lover: A Guide for Gay Men* (Haworth). He received his Master of Social Work degree from NYU and his BA from the State University of New York at Stony Brook. He has written articles on subjects that include gay male relationships, HIV, anti-gay violence, and suicide. Mr. Kaminsky regularly facilitates workshops on gay male relationships at the Gay and Lesbian Center in Los Angeles and also conducts talks on gay male relationships in different parts of the United States. He has a wide range of clinical experience, including working with gay men in private practice, with seniors and others in medical settings, with hospice patients, and with psychiatrically hospitalized individuals. Visit him at his Web site www.neilkaminsky .com.

CONTENTS

Acknowledgments

It's said that writing is a solitary endeavor. Not so, when there's abundant support all around you. Many people were around me while writing this book.

My partner, Virgilio Vergara, is a precious soul. Thanks, first, for existing. Thanks for all the laughing, and caring, and smiling. Thank you for your love and the joy you give. I feel extremely fortunate each morning when I open my eyes and you are there.

My gratitude is expressed to those gay men who were willing to be interviewed for this book. It's not easy to share the most private aspects of one's life, yet these men did it with enthusiasm and honesty and passion. They selflessly gave of their time to tell their stories. They made a major contribution, and I'm inspired and grateful. Thank you.

Betty Berzon, PhD, therapist, and well-known author of a number of books on gay and lesbian relationships, did not hesitate to give me her time and share with me her invaluable knowledge and insight. I had never met Dr. Berzon before my interview with her, and her willingness to contribute is deeply appreciated. With profound regret, I learned that Dr. Berzon died not very long after I interviewed her. My condolences and prayers go to the many people who knew and loved her.

Brian Wolfe, MFT, formerly in private practice in San Francisco, busy, with the flu, and living in New Zealand, answered my call for help. He readily responded to my lengthy e-mail interview. As usual, his comments were perceptive, intelligent, and witty.

Thanks to my colleague Eddie Hernandez, who reviewed some of my writing on interracial/intercultural relationships, and shared his wisdom and feedback on the subject.

Thank you Lance Avington, fellow writer and extremely smart human being, for all the support you give. I've enjoyed our numerous

Man Talk: The Gay Couple's Communication Guide
© 2007 by The Haworth Press, Inc. All rights reserved.
doi:10.1300/5527_a

dinners in West Hollywood where we shared our thoughts and visions about writing. And also a few drinks!

Thank you Gordon Gilbert, for our daily LA/New York conversations. You're a great friend and you gave me some excellent ideas for this book. And you keep me laughing.

Of course, I save the very best for last. Thanks Mom (Gussie Kaminsky), Dad (Louis Kaminsky), and Aunt Tillie (Tillie Young). You're in heaven, but you're with me every day of my life.

Introduction

Coming together with a soul mate is a wonderful, longed-for dream brought to fruition. Having a relationship with him, however, is another story. Scores of gay men spend years chasing love, and the path can be tough and lonely. Sometimes we confuse sex with love, deceit with honesty, and passion with attachment. Occasionally, we even confuse madness with sanity.

When we do finally discover the real, right one, we understandably assume that our arduous journey is over. We have come out of the shadows and can now bask in the resplendent tranquility of love.

If that's what you think, sit down! Take a deep breath. The fun is just about to begin. Prepare to embark on a new journey called "having a relationship that can work."

This journey need not be one of anguish, however. It can actually be far superior to the *dream* of love. It can bring you to levels of contentment and intimacy you never thought possible. This happens when you and your lover can get through to each other. This book is about communication. Communication is not a lost art. It's not difficult to execute, and it can make the difference between happiness and misery, remaining together or breaking up. Sad is when you could have made it if only you had been able to get through to each other. That regret never needs to happen again! You can prevent it *starting right now!*

Man Talk: The Gay Couple's Communication Guide will teach you how to effectively communicate with your lover. It addresses numerous types of communication difficulties between gay men, and provides practical, straightforward strategies to affirmatively transform your relationship.

Man Talk: The Gay Couple's Communication Guide
© 2007 by The Haworth Press, Inc. All rights reserved.
doi:10.1300/5527_01

Explicitly, the book coaches you on how to:

- Say what you mean plainly, clearly, and without hidden agendas
- Avoid communication destroyers like yelling and threatening to break up
- Listen in a manner that enables you to fully understand your partner
- Express anger in a fashion that improves, not erodes your relationship
- Successfully deal with uncomfortable topics such as sex and money
- Understand your feelings and how to articulate them
- Tackle the impediments to communication brought about by male socialization
- Let go of the need to control and be right
- Turn disagreements into problem-solving endeavors, not "courtroom" battles
- Appreciate cultural influences on communication, and how to communicate in bicultural, biracial relationships
- Recognize and comprehend the multilevels of communication
- Communicate love and care and appreciation

Man Talk: The Gay Couple's Communication Guide consists of ten chapters:

1. *"Communication: The Heart of Love"* introduces the main theme of the book, namely that effective communication is essential to any viable relationship. It also touches on principal issues that will be further explored such as anger, feelings, and ways that communication gets derailed.
2. *"Do You Know Your Boyfriend? Misinterpretations That Breed Contempt"* looks at how previous bad experiences with boyfriends and others in your life can haunt your current relationship. For example, if a former boyfriend was dishonest, you may have difficulty trusting your current boyfriend. The chapter elucidates this process, and provides tips on how to distinguish misinterpretations from what is actually going on in your relationship.
3. *"Screaming and Shaming: How to Destroy Communication"* describes the multitude of ways that communication is ob-

structed. This includes, among many others, bringing up multiple past grievances at the same time, disrespect, personal attacks, and passive-aggressive behavior. The chapter describes why these behaviors are destructive, why we engage in them, and strategies to control them.

4. *"Communication Minefields: The Seven Deadly Topics Gay Men Won't Talk About"* explores seven topics (your sexual relationship with your partner, money, sexual interest in others, relationship ambivalence, addictions, open relationships, and insecurity about being loved) that gay men often find difficult to talk about. The chapter speaks to the importance of these issues, the consequences of avoidance, and how to begin a dialogue.

5. *"How to Stop Running from Your Male Feelings"* explores the role of male socialization in rewarding "control" and "strength" at the expense of having access to emotions. It also explores how growing up gay in a homophobic society compounds the problem by socializing us into compartmentalizing feelings of same sex attraction. The necessity of understanding and accepting one's feelings in order to effectively communicate is described. Techniques are provided to help men "de-program" from the need to be "in control" and gain access and tolerance of their feelings.

6. *"Making Peace with Anger"* addresses the confusion and discomfort we have with anger. Anger is identified as a relationship fact of life, and guidance is provided on how to express anger appropriately. The chapter also explores the opposite poles of dysfunctional handling of anger (avoidance of anger or destructive anger; e.g., explosiveness) and why neither can co-exist with effective communication. The issue of physical violence and how it differs from anger is also clarified.

7. *"Silence and the Art of Listening"* explores in detail the elements of skillful listening. Listening is an active and rich process that can help immensely in understanding one's partner. The reader is assisted in accomplishing this by learning how to get the facts straight, steer clear of distractions, and avoid the temptation to advise and "fix." A number of exercises are provided to help the reader improve his listening skills. The

immense importance of "being heard" as a conduit to intimacy is described.

8. *"Cultural Exchange: Communicating in Interracial Relationships"* describes some of the communication challenges in biracial, bicultural relationships. Issues described include family of origin ties, the comfort or discomfort with being out, and the use or avoidance of open discussion to resolve difficulties. The problem of racism is addressed as well as the significance of recognizing the limits of one's knowledge of another culture and the willingness to learn.

9. *"Communication Problems As a Warning Sign: Coming to Terms with Relationship Meltdown"* describes relationships that are in serious trouble and how problems with communication may be at the core of their difficulties. The chapter discusses how to recognize a relationship in serious trouble and what to do to salvage it. The chapter also addresses relationships that are beyond repair, and how communication difficulties may be symptomatic of relationship demise. Couple's therapy and how it can help in both the reparative and uncoupling process is explained.

10. *"Affirmative Communication: Sharing Feelings, Love, and Life"* the final chapter, synthesizes the major points of the book. It focuses on the numerous ways to effectively communicate and create a fulfilling, lasting relationship. From recognizing the gift of having love, to letting him know the magnitude of his presence, this chapter describes what makes happy relationships, and how you can have that in your life.

Use of Vignettes and Quotes

The book uses vignettes, quotes from two psychotherapists who have significant experience working with gay men, and quotes from a number of gay men in relationships. The purpose of using quotes and vignettes is to put real faces on the material while further illustrating certain ideas. All quotes are accurate statements of what was said or written. The identifying information of the gay men (name, age, city, profession) has been changed to protect privacy. The identifying information of the therapists is accurate. The vignettes are purely fictitious, developed from the writer's professional and personal experiences.

Use of the Terms Lover, Boyfriend, Partner, and Soul Mate

Since different folks have different meanings for these terms, I have avoided using one more than others. I don't want to appear to exclude some people. For example, if I consistently used the word "lover" and you refer to your man as your boyfriend, you may think I wasn't referring to your situation. That would be a mistake. I have therefore used the terms more or less interchangeably (soul mate is actually used very little). Whatever I call him, I am referring to the man in your life who you are in love with, who holds a special place in your life, and who you have a romantic relationship with. What you call him is your business.

Disclaimer

This book is written with the aim of improving communication between gay men in relationships. However, no guarantee is claimed nor implied that this will be achieved for any particular individual(s).

I am a licensed clinical social worker in California and all statements made by me are within the scope of my practice as a social worker. No claim is being made nor implied that I have any medical training nor any kind of professional training other than that of a social worker. Neither medical advice nor any other advice out of my scope of practice is being given or implied.

Recommendations and advice provided are not claimed to be nor implied to be comprehensive, appropriate recommendations for any particular individual(s).

Serious issues such as domestic violence, addictions, and mental illness are discussed in this book. The reader is urged to seek competent professional help if he suffers from or believes he may be suffering from any of these conditions.

Absolutely no claim is being made nor implied that this book can be a substitute for psychotherapy, medical intervention, or any other kind of professional help.

Chapter 1

Communication: The Heart of Love

When there's no communication, there's no connection. It's like being in the dark and you can bump into things and you can really hurt yourself and you can really hurt somebody. Communication is like a candle, a bright light, that can illuminate so many things . . .

Aidan, 37, physical therapist
Tampa, Florida

If there is no communication . . . what is the point of being with someone?

Brian Wolfe, MFT
formerly in private practice, San Francisco, CA
(now living in New Zealand)

His arrival is a momentous occasion that awakens the soul. Your new boyfriend is the sparkling center of your now blissful existence. Time apart hurts; time together soars. Talk is effortless and pleasurable. Sex is hot and never enough. As he opens up, you think you know him. You reveal feelings and secrets and he thinks he knows you. You both feel bonded. But are you?

The beginning is exhilarating. But it's not a relationship. It's the outline of what *may arrive*. It's the outer coating, the potential, the possibility. The early days are enchanting, but they are short—very short, on reality. A loving union between two men—a relationship— is both. With reality come challenges, ambivalence, dissatisfaction, and life changes. Love also arrives—*real* love, true caring, intimacy. The requisite path to creating and sustaining a relationship is communication.

Man Talk: The Gay Couple's Communication Guide
© 2007 by The Haworth Press, Inc. All rights reserved.
doi:10.1300/5527_02

7

So What Exactly Is Communication?

To communicate, according to the *Oxford American Dictionary,* is to "make known," "to succeed in conveying information," "to be connected."[1] It's hard to imagine two people in a relationship who are unable to make known what they feel, where information is not being conveyed, and where no feeling of connection exists. In such a situation you may have two people sharing a meal or a life, but they are not sharing a relationship, a sad state of affairs indeed. The good news is that it need not be that way.

More Good News

Being able to communicate effectively is not rocket science. You don't have to possess an innate talent, and I'm fairly confident there is no communication gene. You do have to be open to examining how you relate to your lover, and need to be willing to unlearn some comfortable, but dysfunctional habits. You do have to go within, and learn about yourself and your feelings. It will be a different world than you now know, but a better one!

Letting go of the expectation of the early days when everything was so called "perfect" doesn't mean you have to look ahead to unending analysis and conversations that go deep into the night. On the contrary, effective communication is about being in sync, not talking through and processing everything to death. Effective communication means more quality and less quantity of discourse. Effective communication will cut out the time and energy squandered on arguing and dancing around issues. It will shorten the recovery period after a bad fight. Indeed, it will minimize the likelihood of having a blowout in the first place. Not communicating means interminable discussion, expression of rage and reciprocal defensiveness, along with blame for "sins" committed as far back as Galileo! This is horrific, time-consuming drudgery that gets you absolutely nowhere. Effective communication means addressing and resolving issues. It means expressing love and caring and validation. It's a lot less work, a lot more fun, and it has no downside.

---

[1]Ehrlich, Eugene et al., *Oxford American Dictionary,* New York: Avon Books, 1982, pp. 170-171.

Loneliness

One of the most significant reasons we bond in adult relationships is to feel connected, to thwart off loneliness. Effective communication is requisite for that to happen. When you aren't communicating, you will feel lonely, because in a very real sense you are alone. That is extremely frustrating and raises the question of why you are together at all. Feeling lonely in a relationship is usually a sign of serious communication breakdown.

Intimacy and Feelings

Intimacy is the heart of a relationship. It's the capacity to get close and feel safe with another human being, and ability to strip off social masks and be authentic. It's the experience of sharing triumphs and disappointments. When lovers are able to do this, there is potential for great happiness. Effective communication is the road to this happiness. It's the way you are able to express what you are about and understand where he's coming from. This implies emotional availability and support, and implies an understanding *of feelings: communication is in very large part the expression and acceptance of feelings without judgment.* Thus, you may be upset that your lover was promoted while you remain trapped in an unhappy job. Feeling upset doesn't mean you want your lover to be miserable or that you are a jealous, "bad" human being. It simply means you have a feeling. Being able to communicate this directly and being heard by your lover without scorn builds that closeness.

To do this is not as easy as saying it, however. We often confuse feelings with actions. We demand feelings to be logical. We see "bad" feelings as evidence of personality flaws. We live in a judgment-obsessed society, and view *not* being critical of feelings as unnatural and disingenuous.

> . . . In my family you were not supposed to express any feelings unless you could justify them, especially the negative feelings.
>
> Harvey, 42, physician
> Cleveland, Ohio

Learning to communicate is creating a whole new understanding and relationship with your feelings and others' feelings.

Access to Feelings

Feelings are infinitely complex. Similar to dreams, they can be terribly illogical, and competing; opposing feelings can exist simultaneously. As in the above example, you may be happy for your lover, angry at him for having it "so easy," jealous because your situation is bad, hopeful because if that can happen to him maybe it will happen to you, and guilty for not having only pure goodwill. These feelings can come at warp speed and you may only be aware that you are confused.

Uncomfortable feelings may be particularly difficult to access. Painful feelings can be covered over by denial, destructive behavior, or secondary feelings that derail communication.

Rage is an example of a secondary feeling. Your partner tells you that he is uninterested in you sexually. He is demanding that the relationship be opened. You react with screaming, and tell him that he's a loathsome ingrate. Are you really angry, or are you hurt, saddened, and frightened? Although we don't know the whole story (perhaps he's telling you this in an insulting tone), his words wound. They also threaten; they are telling you that a principal understanding between the two of you has to be changed, with all the accompanying distress, unnavigated terrain, and danger. Furthermore they create self-esteem assault. He is seeking others who will satisfy him because you don't.

These feelings of hurt, sadness, fear, vulnerability, and ego deflation are much more painful than rage, *in the short run*. They make you feel out of control; rage gives you the *illusion, in the moment,* of having control. Thus, your mind may go to instant fury without even being aware of these other, much more significant emotions.

Sometimes this also results in destructive behavior. You begin an affair. You'll show him. Two can play at this game! No talk, no addressing what is really going on between the two of you—just an affair that evens the score and makes you feel desirable. Or you tell him fine, case closed. Go ahead and enjoy yourself. You feel nothing.

None of this is effective communication. Effective communication is learning how to slow down the process and retrieve and address the more uncomfortable emotions. It's about avoiding destructive behavior to cover up pain. It's about understanding that feelings are often illogical, and to embrace that reality. It's about appreciating that feeling nothing is feeling something, and that it's imperative to find out what it is.

Men and Feelings

While women don't exclusively own the rights to insight, men, as a group, have a more difficult experience with understanding and dealing with feelings. Stereotypes aside that gay men are more sensitive, etc., we are still men socialized in a society in which big boys don't cry. We are apt to be less aware of what we feel, and more ready to charge into action than sit back and try to figure out what is going on. As gay couples made up of two men, this can be a volatile situation as each man refuses to be the first to blink.

Men often don't take kindly to the expression of feelings, and a fear exists, sometimes quite correctly, that serious consequences may occur if we let our feelings be known.

> ... I knew that there was the chance that I would lose the relationship if I spoke up; if I said what I was feeling it could cost the relationship. And it took me a month to deal with that. Ultimately it did cost the relationship, but I at least felt like I put it out there. It still hurt, and it still sucked ...
>
> Danny, 31, teacher
> Austin, Texas

Aaron and Donald

Aaron and Donald live in San Francisco. On a Sunday afternoon in the late fall they took a day trip to the Napa Valley north of the city. Donald had eaten a great deal of junk food the previous Saturday night and was feeling ill. He kept complaining about his upset stomach and lack of energy. This garnered anger from Aaron rather than sympathy. He felt Donald had been irresponsible and now blamed him for ruining their day.

Both men had legitimate issues. Donald should not have overindulged with food and his choice did negatively affect their day together. But he didn't plan to ruin anything and he was now actually ill.

Aaron would certainly not want Donald to be ill but was unhappy that his enjoyment was being compromised. Had both men been able to express their feelings in a safe and receptive environment (*Aaron:* I feel frustrated that you are ill because of what you ate last night; enjoying this day to the fullest means a lot to me. *Donald:* Yes, I made a mistake but I am very nauseous right now; it seems that you don't care how bad I feel) there would have been an understanding and less tension. It would not cure the problem of Donald's illness but they would not be arguing, making the day considerably more ruined. Unfortunately each man became lost in his own righteousness, resulting in a lot of hard feelings and a blowup that really did ruin the day.

They had just visited the Coppola winery, owned by the famous director Francis Ford Coppola, when all hell broke loose. The following conversation ensued:

DONALD: Let's not go to another winery. I can't drink anything and I feel nauseous.

AARON: Who asked you to eat all that crap last night? My God, you ate a half a gallon of ice cream. And all that other shit.

DONALD: Okay, you're right. I was stupid, but I feel sick now.

AARON: Oh, I'm sorry to hear that. But why don't you get sick on your own time? You know how hard I've been working lately and how badly I need a little fun. So now I am supposed to drop everything just because you're not feeling well?

DONALD: I'm not saying let's go home. I just don't want to run around so much. Why don't we sit out here and relax for a while. This winery is a beautiful place.

AARON: No. When I go up to Napa I like to visit a number of wineries and do tasting. You know that. Now I have to sit here and do nothing? You're ruining this day.

DONALD: *Aaron, I am feeling ill. Do you hear me?* I am ill. I could throw up.

AARON: You should have thought of that yesterday when you pigged out.

DONALD: For crying out loud, you stupid selfish bastard. You care more about your fucking wineries than you care about me.

AARON: That's it. This day is over. I work hard all week and now I have to put up with this? Let's go home. The day is ruined.

DONALD: Fine. Let's go home. You ruined it.

AARON: No, you did.

Not a fun afternoon! Have you had an experience like this? I would assume many readers have.

You need experience this no longer. In this book you will learn how to access and appropriately express feelings, so that problems can be managed, not aggravated.

Problem Solving, Not Winning

The goal of winning instead of solving a problem needs to be relinquished if you and your partner are going to communicate with one another. The not-so-hidden agenda rooted in much conflict between lovers is the aim to "win," to be "right," to prevail. That's fine in a court of law but not in your home. Nothing gets solved when you shame your lover into appreciating what a stupid jerk he has been. That only builds a defensive wall. It's an ego assault that will prime him to search for and pounce on any semblance of wrongness you exhibit in the future (which may be in the next hour). Focusing on winning is a lose/lose situation. It's the antithesis to problem solving.

To give this up means to buy into the importance of problem solving. This is not an issue in the very beginning because few problems need to be solved. A real relationship spanning the years means multiple problems. Viability means having the tools to resolve them. Effective communication is one of the most important tools.

Anger

Anger is literally nonexistent in the very beginning. This status, however, is *impossible* to sustain over the long haul. Lovers who proclaim that they *never* get angry with each other are not telling the whole story. They may be in denial, they may fear conflict, their relationship may exist at arm's length, or reserves of rage may be waiting to explode one unhappy day. Or there may be various combinations of these examples. None of this is healthy, desirable, or ultimately workable.

Anger happens because people are human, have conflicts, and hurt each other. Sometimes the hurt is intentional and mean spirited, yet at other times the damage is done without intent. The longer a couple is together, the more opportunity occurs for such events. Yearning for a "cruise-control" sense of those early days is wholly unrealistic.

Insensitivity, mistakes, or downright occasional meanness doesn't have to be the end of the world or the end of the relationship. But the problem(s) must be addressed and resolved; each man must feel heard. If anger is present, the feelings must be verbally expressed and accepted. If the hurt and angry feelings can be openly communicated, the problems have the highest likelihood of being resolved.

Anger is a very difficult emotion for most people. It's uncomfortable, it's not pretty, it doesn't feel loving, and it's often confused with violence and destruction. Anger can be highly destructive when out of control. However, out of control anger also includes passive-aggressive behavior in which anger is expressed indirectly. Example: Your lover embarrasses you in front of a friend during dinner. You say nothing then or later. The next day you need to transfer your share of money into the joint account in order to pay the mortgage. You "forget" and the check bounces.

Effective communication allows anger to have it's rightful place without destroying anything. We are going to learn how to express anger without avoidance, violence, or causing lasting hurt.

Going Away by Itself

A benign rash may come and go and your life is none the worse. But a rash that goes away may also be syphilis, and not seeing the doctor will make your life a whole lot worse.

Major problems in a relationship do not self-destruct. They are often scary to confront head on, so when they are avoided the short-term calm can mislead one to believe that everything will be okay. But it won't. The specific nonaddressed event will have no closure, and the dynamics leading to the problem remain the same. Trouble than repeats itself in different forms and tends to escalate exponentially and destroy a relationship.

Jeffrey and Michael

Jeffrey and Michael lived in Los Angeles and had been a couple for two years. They had tickets to see Bette Midler in concert on a Tuesday evening at the Staples Center in Los Angeles. That evening turned into a relationship-changing disaster.

Michael had been working very long hours for the past year. He was a regional manager for a foreign exchange bank whose headquarters were in Paris. He often worked fifteen-hour days and some weekends. On four different occasions in the past six months Michael had to travel to Paris. The trips usually came with less than twenty-four hours notice, and any plans they made were quashed as his job took priority.

The situation was stressful for both men, but Michael accepted this as part of the job and never questioned what choice he would make. Although he assumed his work schedule was stressful for Jeffrey, he didn't think it was a big deal for him. He was quite wrong. Jeffrey became increasingly disenchanted and began to hope that Michael would somehow lose his job. *But he said nothing.* He was frightened to address the possibility that a fundamental conflict existed between Michael's career and their relationship. So each time Michael was called away or burned the midnight oil Jeffrey stuffed his feelings and hoped for the best. He didn't get it.

During the times that Michael was in Paris Jeffrey began spending time with Kevin, a guy he met in a local Starbucks. Jeffrey felt comforted by Kevin's attention, and couldn't help fantasizing about a sexual relationship with him. But he kept it platonic despite mutual flirtation and sexual tension. He had a monogamous agreement with Michael, and he wasn't going to do anything to threaten their future.

That is, until the evening of the Bette Midler concert. At 4 p.m. on the day of the concert Michael called Jeffrey to tell him that he had to finish a report that would need to reach Paris by the next day. He couldn't make the concert and he apologized, suggesting that Jeffrey take a friend. He would make it up to him next week by taking him to a fancy dinner in Beverly Hills.

Guess who went to the concert with Jeffrey? Guess who didn't come home that night? At 3 a.m. Michael called the police. They told him they couldn't do anything until Jeffrey was missing twenty-four hours. At 7 a.m. Jeffrey finally called Michael, who was terrified, exhausted, and confused.

"What on earth is going on? Where are you? Are you okay?"

"How's the fucking report coming?" Jeffrey answered.

"What . . . what the hell is going on, Jeff? Where in God's name are you? Have you been drinking?"

"Did you finish your sorry-ass report?"

". . . What . . . are you on something? What the fuck is going on, goddam it?"

"What's going on?" Jeffrey responded, "I just fucked my friend Kevin and you can go to hell."

Jeffrey then hung up.

Not only did the first problem not go away, but it grew into a monster crisis and gave birth to a new, very serious dilemma. Had Jeffrey expressed his feelings earlier, Michael may have made different choices. Certainly the anger in Jeffrey would not have built as it did and there would have been an opportunity to find a solution. Perhaps a solution wouldn't be found, but saying nothing *guaranteed* that. While it can be argued that Michael was insensitive to Jeffrey, Jeffrey still had a responsibility to communicate his distress. Michael had no way to know *just what his unavailability meant to Jeffrey, how Jeffrey actually felt* unless Jeffrey communicated it.

Anxiety and Intimacy

Getting close is a two-edged sword, wonderfully fulfilling yet intensely scary. As you go from the early stage of infatuation to love and commitment, a feeling of loss of freedom arises. Suddenly decisions involve a second person. Accountability and responsibility to another human being did not exist when you were single. Mental health professionals sometimes call this feeling *engulfment,* which is a good description of the psychological state. Engulfment denotes a sense of being swallowed up; no one in his right mind wants such a feeling.

Of course no one is being consumed. But if you *feel* engulfed, what are you likely to do? Probably run! Such feelings bring many relationships to an end just as intimacy is beginning to develop.

> . . . if I get very affectionate in a very genuine deep feeling way . . . I want to run away. I feel myself really starting to close down.
>
> Harvey, 42, physician
> Cleveland, Ohio

Being aware of these feelings and being able to talk about them can prevent a premature dissolution. The following dialogue exemplifies such a situation. Arnold and Gavin have been together for six months.

Arnold and Gavin

ARNOLD: So, are you going to sleep over at my house tonight?

GAVIN: Actually, I'm not.

ARNOLD: No?

GAVIN: No . . . I need to see my own bed. I haven't been home in three nights.

ARNOLD: But . . . being together has been fun, hasn't it?

GAVIN: Totally.

ARNOLD: So what's wrong? Is something wrong? You don't care about me?

GAVIN: Arnold . . . I care a lot about you. But I think this is getting a little too intense. I want some time alone . . . some time to be by myself. I get this feeling I am losing *me* when we spend so much time together. That is scaring me. . . . I can't explain this better.

ARNOLD: Oh, I understand what you're saying. And I definitely don't want to scare you.

GAVIN: Thank you.

ARNOLD: So we are still okay? You mean it's not that you are feeling different toward me? That you still feel good about us. Just need a little more space?

GAVIN: That's exactly it! I'm not talking about breaking up. I'm not going anywhere. Just need some space to feel more balanced. I am very excited about you and me and don't want to kill it by overdoing it!

ARNOLD: "Overdo." I like that term. You know I hate to be without you. But you've got a point that actually makes *me* feel good. I've been thinking about it myself. I need some down time also. I haven't seen my friend Tom in two weeks, and let's not even talk about what's happened to my laundry! I think some of this space will be good for me too. . . . Just not too much [laughing].

GAVIN: Only a little.

ARNOLD: Okay. Let me help you get your stuff together so you can go.

GAVIN: Thanks . . . . Thanks for being understanding.

Life Changes

All of us go through major changes as adults, many of them unwelcome. We may have a financial crisis, become seriously ill, or question who we are and where we are going in life. Sometimes multiple challenges come all at once and it's easy to feel overwhelmed. This puts tremendous stress on a relationship, and the only way for the couple to prevail is to be able to understand each other and be able to cope with the discomfort. This includes giving one's partner space to *not* discuss his feelings at times, and to recognize that he himself may not be able to fully understand what is happening.

Effective communication enables one to wait through such dark times and not feel isolated. If you understand that your lover needs space, you won't experience at as rejection or being cut off. You will understand that it's about him, not you. He will experience the space as being respectful and insightful about his needs.

During crisis, we also need to be comforted both physically and emotionally. If the two of you are able to communicate, you will be able to give him comfort when he needs it, and he will be able to accept it for what it is—support, not taking over.

Misinterpretation

The wish to understand and be understood by your lover, with all the aforementioned gains, often does not match the actuality of communication. Countless paths to communication hell are paved with the best intentions. One sure road is misinterpretation: hearing what he has *not* said, concluding what he does *not* mean, and reacting to what is *not* happening. In the next chapter we explore this maddening confusion, and learn how to better perceive what your boyfriend really means.

Chapter 2

Do You Know Your Boyfriend? Misinterpretations That Breed Contempt

Many of us maintain the strange belief that the only version of reality is the one we have! An individual speaks rapidly and you conclude that he's excited. Your friend says he's angry and another person observes fear. But unless the person tells you how he's feeling, all of this is conjecture.

There is no pure "out there." This is best illustrated with eyewitnesses to a crime. Five people see the same act and yet five different versions may be related of what happened. Is anyone lying? Unlikely. Each individual perceived the event differently.

Perception is very complicated and influenced by many factors. Chief among them are previous experiences and the kind of beliefs developed from those experiences. "Previous" can be as remote as childhood, and yet recent, as in prior significant relationships.

Beliefs and coming to rapid conclusions and actions based on those beliefs are essential for survival. They give us a framework from which we navigate the world. If every time you crossed the street you had to develop the belief that you were in danger, and then had to figure out a safety strategy and put it into action (look before you cross, wait for the light to change, judge how far an oncoming car is away), your chances of being killed would be high.

Assumptions and actions based on strong beliefs get us in trouble when the match to the outside world is not forthcoming. This is not rare, particularly in romantic relationships. Your ex who was screwing when he was supposed to be in night school doesn't mean your current boyfriend is planning a tryst when he leaves for the weekend to visit his ill grandma. But how do you know? It may feel like the

Man Talk: The Gay Couple's Communication Guide
© 2007 by The Haworth Press, Inc. All rights reserved.
doi:10.1300/5527_03

same thing. If you accuse him of such when in fact the trip is all about being with his beloved grandmother, trouble is imminent.

> I was involved in a relationship ten years ago where I ended up paying for a lot more than my fair share . . . so in this relationship when I see anything that looks like that . . . a financial issue that I may have to take care of, even though it's in a whole new context, I immediately go "oh great, here we go again."

> Harvey, 42, physician
> Cleveland, Ohio

Body and Other Language

Sometimes misperceptions come in the form of how we perceive language, the tone of speech or body communication. Your boyfriend is preoccupied with a personal worry (he got a speeding ticket); you interpret his spacey look as disinterest in what you are saying. Your boyfriend tells you on the phone from work "I want to talk with you tonight—it's important—can't get into it right now." You interpret that something is seriously amiss, but in fact he wants to speak with you about hiring a cleaning person because neither of you have much time to do it.

Your assumptions may come from his behavior in the past or from similar behavior with others. Maybe a former lover spoke to you in this manner just before he announced that he was leaving.

Trauma-Based Assumptions

Misinterpretations can be more complicated as in the following vignette:

Benjamin and Sam

Benjamin, on more than one occasion, had given what Sam considered the "third degree" about what he had done when they were not together. Ben would ask a lot of detailed questions. In fact, he was simply curious and actually thought this proved his concern about Sam. He did *not* distrust him, but Sam had come out of a relationship a year previously with a man who demanded to know everything he did when they were apart, even when he left the house to go to the grocery for thirty minutes. When Benjamin began with his questions on one cool San Francisco evening, Sam's response was swift and clear.

"Don't give me the third degree; don't give me this shit. Keep this up and you're not going to have a boyfriend."

Flabbergasted and confused, Benjamin tried to tell Sam that he simply wanted to know whether or not he had a nice day. Sam shot back.

"Sure, you just want to make sure that your little boyfriend is being a good boy. Well, you don't own me and I don't have to account for my time. I'm not going to be controlled by anyone."

Benjamin felt confused and angry. The idea of being attacked for innocent questions that *he* thought were actually sweet did not sit well with him. He grew more frustrated.

"Sam, I'm not trying to do any of what you're accusing me of. Where this bug up your ass came from beats me. I just wanted to know how your damn day went. Sorry for being interested in your life."

"Sure you're interested in my life. This is how it always starts. You do not own me Benjamin, and don't lie to me. Don't ask me those kinds of questions ever again. *Case closed.*"

Wow!

Benjamin is not concerned about infidelity or control but Sam's previous experience has created the unquestionable belief that this kind of behavior means just that. It's also experienced by Sam as intrusion, distrust, being monitored, and needing to account for his time. This would be a dreadful way to live and a legitimate reason to respond—*if it were true.* The sad fact is they're headed for trouble because of *absolutely nothing.* Nothing really bad is going on except for what is in Sam's head.

So how can this be diffused?

If you're having a disagreement in which each of you are seeing the same issue in a very different light, it's likely that powerful beliefs are involved. As difficult at it may feel, it's imperative that you both work on cooling down in the moment and find out what each of you is experiencing.

Both of you must buy in that you have something to talk about in a civilized manner. If emotions are white hot, both of you should take a few minutes of time out to take the edge off. Walk in another room for a couple of minutes or take a walk outside for ten minutes. *But then come back and start communicating.*

How? The following example illustrates this.

BENJAMIN: Let's calm down . . . both of us. Sorry about the bug up your ass comment. You and I are seeing this very differently. We need to talk.

SAM: I still think we have nothing to talk about.

BENJAMIN: If we're having such a big disagreement and seeing this in such opposite ways, I think we need to clear the air.

SAM: So what do you want to talk about?

BENJAMIN: You apparently are very sensitive to my questions. But this is the fact: I trust you. I would not stay with you if I didn't. My questions are really innocent. I just wanted to know how your day went today.

SAM: Hershel drove me crazy with this stuff. He wanted to know everything I did. I felt that I didn't have my own life. And now you're starting that.

BENJAMIN: But I'm not. I'm not Hershel. I trust you. You don't need to account to me.

SAM: But you keep asking me questions.

BENJAMIN: For different reasons.

SAM: So why does it feel that you're investigating me?

BENJAMIN: I'm not sure, but I guess if that happened with Herschel you are assuming it's happening with me. I could imagine how horrible that could feel. I wouldn't stand for it. I wouldn't want to have to account to someone for my time. I gave that up at seventeen with my mother. But when I asked you if you had fun with Sherry at lunch, I wanted to know that you had a good time. She always cracks you up and I love to see you laughing. This had nothing to do with accounting for your time.

SAM: Well, she did crack me up. She got down and dirty and I almost spit up my lunch!

BENJAMIN: Great! I don't mean great that you almost barfed!

SAM: But back to the problem. How do I know you're not going to turn into Herschel? I mean Herschel seemed innocent at first and he turned into a nightmare.

BENJAMIN: Well, I'm not Herschel. Remember the name is Benjamin, not Herschel. They don't even sound the same! And maybe with more time you'll actually see that it won't happen. But if you're feeling that a question is intrusive, it's fine to tell me that. Just tell me how you feel. Don't start accusing me of all kinds of stuff.

SAM: Well, okay, I'll try that. But I don't know if it's going to work. I have a real sore spot from what I went through with Herschel.

BENJAMIN: I know. I understand.

It's likely that this will come up again. Sam's experience with Herschel has been deeply unsettling. But the real issue is on the table. Benjamin understands Sam's feelings and Sam is in touch with the effect that Hershel has had on him.

Core Misinterpretations

Some previous experiences create primary perceptions and styles of relating with the world. I'm referring to the thousands of interactions with parents (or parental figures), other important adults (e.g., teachers), and peers that shape your outlook on life. They especially format your understanding and expectations of intimate relationships. A characteristic example is the adult hearing himself articulate the same words that were said to him by his parents. Like it or not, these formative occurrences create bedrock blueprints of how we relate as adults.

No parental influence is devoid of problems because parents are human. However, the less chaos in a family, the less problems with adult intimacy. Boundary violation, manipulation, neglect, and abuse are likely to produce formidable challenges.

Child "Adults"

An all too common and unfortunate story are children who play the role of pseudo adult to their parents. Sometimes this involves parents who abuse alcohol and/or other drugs. Other times the parents are mentally ill. Pseudoadult children also exist in families with less dramatic dysfunction.

Such a child is one who assumes responsibilities that are inappropriate and beyond his capacity to effectively execute. The shared psychological dynamic of such children is the focus on the care/welfare/feeling states, etc., of others at the expense of their own needs. One man described this to me as "raising my parents well."

A child adult looks for his drunken daddy in an alleyway, or who tries to make peace between his bickering parents. It's the ten-year-old who parents his four-year-old brother. It's the girl who feels responsible for her mother's depression, and the boy who skips baseball to keep his lonely mother company. It's all the children who try in vain to put their Humpty-Dumpty families back together again.

More or less, these children miss out on having a childhood. Some also miss out on having an adulthood. Such folks may continue this kind of relationship throughout their lives. They never stop seeing themselves as the little boy or girl who must make Mommy and Daddy happy. They remain enmeshed and continue to take responsibility for that which is not their responsibility. A gay man hides his orientation because it "will kill my mother." A woman won't leave the old neighborhood because "my parents need me." A man plays the role of peacemaker because "I want them to get along" (even though they never did).

All of this creates resentment. Bottomless resentment. To make matters worse, the person I'm describing often doesn't have a clue about how this role has affected him, how he continues to keep the role alive, and how this will affect his relationship with his lover. All he knows is that he's angry. Chronically angry. Ragefully angry. Anger that will find a direct path to his lover.

What do I mean?

A relationship with a lover is psychologically similar in intensity to a relationship with a parent. Both are deep, powerful connections. The adult relationship reminds the individual, on an emotional level, of this earliest and most basic relationship. This is universal. We all have feelings toward our partners that originate from and become confused with our feelings toward our parents. Much of this is benign.

You may see your lover as deeply nurturing because your mom is nurturing. He may be a great guy yet not as selfless. Nevertheless, there's no problem here. It is a distortion but at worst he gets a little more credit than he deserves. You're both happy. Case closed.

Perhaps your dad is a stickler for being on time so you get a little annoyed when your lover reminds you not to be late for the dentist. Your annoyance is a distortion because it's your father, not your lover, who's the perfectionist. Your partner just wants to make certain your teeth get fixed. Again this is no cause for concern.

The same cannot be said for rage. Rage is irrational, explosive energy. It creates a distressing feeling that craves pain-inflicting expression. It doesn't manifest as a sober discussion ("You know, Dino, I realize you have destroyed my life so let's talk about this") but rather as an exploding projectile. The recipient of that missile, your partner, will have a less than welcome response. This can occur in a variety of ways.

Real Similarities

The partner of such an individual may possess some of the characteristics of his abusive parents. More often than not, we seek out partners that are similar in ways to a parent (or parents) even if that person was no good for us.

This lover may expect, even demand care like his parents did. But even though he is similar, *he is not his parent. He was not there hurting him* when he was small. He is not vulnerable with him as he was with his parents.

The rage he feels is embedded unconsciously in those feelings of victimization and powerlessness. When he lashes out at his partner for ordering him to do the laundry when he wants to take a nap, he's not upset about laundry. He's feeling ordered to abdicate his needs as *he really had to* do as a child.

You may say this is not based on reason. Surly he can tell the difference between yesterday and today. Not psychologically. Feelings, especially powerful ones, override reason.

Volunteer Caregivers

Often the child adult initiates the role of caregiver with his partner. He volunteers to carry his weight and then some. It's familiar role and it feels safe. Soon, however, the rage associated with that role comes out fighting.

Billy and Kevin

Billy has a revelation as he's making dinner (while Kevin is in the gym) that he's being used. "Why should I be doing all the work while Kevin has all the fun?" he asks himself. When Kevin returns home he walks into an ambush.

KEVIN: Hi hon, what are you making for dinner?

BILLY: You left your pants on the couch.

KEVIN: Okay, I'm sorry. I forgot . . .

BILLY: I'm tired of living in a pigpen. I'm not your maid.

KEVIN: I didn't say you were. I'll pick up . . .

BILLY: You always say that and then you do nothing. I take care of everything around here and you do nothing.

KEVIN: Now wait a minute. What's bugging you? Everything was fine when I left to go to the gym.

BILLY: Nothing is fine.

KEVIN: What's bugging you? Something is definitely bugging you.

BILLY: Now you're telling me what I'm thinking,

KEVIN: What? . . . I'm just trying to . . .

BILLY: Make you own dinner. I'm going out.

Stranger Reactions

Rage can manifest in the most innocent situations.

(John is leaving to go to work).
LLOYD: Give me a kiss, John.
JOHN: Don't tell me what to do.

The psychological experience in all these situations is the feeling of being forced to abdicate one's needs for another, of being used, taken advantage of, and manipulated with no way out. This is the heart and soul of this form of misinterpretation.

Core communication misinterpretations take many forms; rage associated with child adult family dynamics is only one. All of them create significant challenges to couples. Among them are believing (with no objective evidence) that your lover:

- Is untrustworthy
- Is lying
- Wants to control you
- Will ultimately leave you
- Doesn't respect you
- Doesn't understand you
- Believes you're a fool
- Is infantilizing you
- Believes you're incompetent
- Hates you when he is angry with you
- Will physically strike you when angry
- Doesn't find you physically attractive
- Has no confidence in you
- Is with you only because of what he can get from you
- Is up to something evil when he's nice to you
- Wants your money
- Can do better than being with you
- Is more popular, better liked, more desired, more successful, etc., than you can ever be

Combinations of these issues may be operating. For example, you may believe that your lover doesn't respect you, has no confidence in you, and is only with you because of what he can get from you (whatever that may be).

Keep in mind that each partner may be experiencing core misinterpretations, making communication exceedingly muddled. The core misinterpretation in one partner can aggravate the same kind of problem in the other. Example: Rex has issues with disrespect while Ronald struggles with feeling incompetent. Annoyed that the vacuum cleaner won't work, and knowing that Ronald used it last, Rex asks Ronald sarcastically "What did you do to it?" Perceiving this as an accusation of incompetence, and embarrassed by it, Ronald stares at the television set and ignores Rex. Rex views this as disrespect and rage associated with that sore spot rapidly materializes. In short order communication is a distant memory. Neither man can appreciate what is going on in the other, and each is lost in his own psychological angst. This predicament is a relationship deal breaker; it guarantees chronic conflict, discord, and eventually burnout.

How Do You Know These Are Misinterpretations?

What if your lover really doesn't respect you? What if he wants to control you? How do you tell the difference between false impressions and actuality? This is not easy, and if there is anything that may require therapy to untangle relationship confusion, this is it. But before you go running out to a therapist, you should do a number of things.

First, and perhaps the most difficult, is to calm down. Emotions are going to be fired up with these issues, and if you are angry it's going to be impossible to think clearly. I recommend doing some soul searching *not* in the presence of your lover. Take a day off from him, not a half- hour. Go to the beach or the mountains or whatever environment will help you relax and reflect. I also recommend bringing a pen and a diary. Writing out and reading one's thoughts often augment thinking.

The first question you need to ask yourself is, What am I feeling? What am I experiencing inside when I get so upset with him? I want to emphasize that I'm asking you to identify your feelings at this juncture, *not your thoughts*. Ironically, thoughts often interfere with gaining access to feelings. Force yourself, if necessary, to turn off that internal chatter and Judge Judy and simply focus on your visceral experience. Your feelings are not right, wrong, good, bad, or ugly. They are just feelings.

After you have identified these emotions, return to your cognitive powers. Ask yourself if any of these painful feelings seem familiar. Other questions could include: Do I often have these feelings with others? Did I have them when I was growing up? Did I feel disrespected, invalidated, taken advantage of? What was occurring then? Did my mother criticize me when I did poorly in school? Did she ignore my accomplishments? Did peers make fun of me? Did they hit me, reject me, and ridicule the way I looked? Did my parents lie to me? When Dad was angry did he strike me?

As you are doing this, put the feelings into categories. For example, if your parents chronically lied to you, the category would be *distrust of those close to me.* If your father physically struck you when he was angry, the category would be *fear of physical assault when someone is angry with me.* Now reflect on your relationship. Do you find similar categories in your feelings toward your partner? For example, do you fear physical assault when he's irate? Then ask yourself, has he actually hit me (*not* screamed at me and said miserable things to me) but *physically struck me?* If he has never hit you, never tried to hit you, never threatened to hit you, but you have lived in fear of violence, this is likely an example of this form of psychological distortion.

This is not to say that verbal abuse is appropriate or something you shouldn't be genuinely concerned about, but it is different from physical violence.

Your goal is to examine memories of feelings and experiences and *empirical evidence* in the present that may or may not produce such feelings. While reality, as previously indicated is relative, empirical evidence is an attempt to minimize subjective interpretation. Simplistically put, empirical evidence means external behavior that can be observed and measured using agreed upon criteria. A slap in the face is external behavior that can be observed and quantified. You can agree that a hand going across a face in a particular manner is a slap and you can observe it (and quantify the force and number of times) if necessary. If he is disrespectful that is a subjective impression that may or not be supported by observable behavior. Cursing you in public is observable evidence of that impression. Appearing somewhere else psychologically on one occasion while you are speaking is not.

If no observable evidence exists and your feelings toward him fit into a known category from the past, it's very likely you are distorting what is happening in the present.

Another matter to consider is the intensity of your reactions to his behavior. For example, if he reminds you to pick up clothes at the cleaners, do you tell him to shut up or go to hell (or both)? If he wants to verify a bill at a restaurant that you just paid, do you explode? Do you think your reaction is appropriate to the situation? If you were able to look at the circumstances as an outside objective observer, what would you think?

Being reminded to pick up your clothes or rechecking a bill can be helpful or unnecessary and annoying. It can be irritating. But it doesn't create fury and significant emotional distress. Such a reaction means the stimulus is coming from somewhere else. That somewhere else is inside you. And that means distortion is occurring.

In a situation as this, I would ask you to think carefully about what you're thinking. Are you telling yourself "He believes I'm an idiot; he's insulting me. He's calling me a moron. He doesn't think I know how to do anything"?

I would also examine my gut. Do you feel put down, embarrassed, stupid, infantilized, incompetent, not trusted? Are these familiar feelings? Do they fall within a category of feelings that you have been struggling with throughout your life?

This kind of scrutiny can be done with any reactions that appear out of proportion to the trigger. If you're having difficulty determining if you are overreacting, ask a friend who can be objective. Objectivity is key. Your friend will be doing you no favor by taking your side if you're distorting reality.

As I mentioned previously, you should ask yourself if you have similar kinds of reactions with others. Similar reactions are important clues. While we are most vulnerable and react most intensely with a lover, core misinterpretations do manifest across the board. If you tend, for example, to feel embarrassed and put down by friends whenever you are corrected, and you explode at your lover for similar behavior, this is something to look at closely.

Still another area to evaluate is the frequency you are getting upset with minor issues. Having numerous disagreements over matters that appear trivial is another sign that the reactions may not related to the obvious. You need to step back from the content of your distress (he left a dish in the sink; he didn't turn out the light; he didn't say thank you) and view the big picture. Am I getting upset too often over matters that an objective observer would consider trivial? I would then look for underlying themes. In the previous example, one could make the argument that there is a theme of "he doesn't care; he doesn't respect me." Then comes the hard part: Are these just his annoying habits that have nothing to do with me, or does it really mean he doesn't care about me? Is this a hot button issue for me? When have I felt like this before? With whom? Do I have other evidence of disrespect? Is it evidence?

Keep in mind that annoying habits, if that's what it is, are legitimate matters to address. You need to be clear whether you're reacting to that or something else, and if that something else is a distortion. Real issues have the potential of being resolved with your lover. Distortions, unless you understand that they are distortions, do not.

Therapy

Fundamental conflicts from early in life are difficult to access and understand. Trauma, even as an adult, can be colored with so much emotion that it becomes impossible to make sense of it. The intersection of reality and distortion, and understanding what is what, is also a formidable challenge. Sometimes an objective professional is needed to untangle this.

If you decide to see a therapist, I'd recommend seeking individual rather than couples therapy. Understanding your particular history and how this affects your current relationships requires a focus on you in the comfort of a safe, nonjudgmental atmosphere. Couples therapy can be helpful with communication, but if you are in the dark about what you're bringing to the table, you are not likely to get very far.

This, of course is only a general recommendation. A competent therapist will understand your particular situation and is in the best position to make recommendations that address your particular best interests. But be clear about his recommendations and make certain you agree with them. A good therapeutic relationship implies the facility to openly discuss your feelings. If you don't agree with the therapist, let him know and have a frank discussion about it.

Bountiful Communication Roadblocks

Distortion, unfortunately, is only one of numerous paths to communication dysfunction. Emotions run strong and deep when you're in love. Because he matters so much, what he says and does, and does not say or do, weighs heavily on your emotions. When there's conflict, which is inevitable, uncomfortable feelings materialize. Those feelings can create a communication nightmare if they're not balanced with thought and good judgment. Screaming when you're furious, lying when you're embarrassed, or plotting revenge when offended, will obstruct communication and resolve nothing. Yet these are behaviors we gravitate to when there's discord. In the next chapter we will explore the numerous ways this manifests, and how communication can be maintained no matter how pissed off both of you are.

Chapter 3

Screaming and Shaming: How to Destroy Communication

An unfortunate fact of human behavior is the facility with which communication can be derailed. Throw in a nasty remark or raise your voice and your partner stops listening. Assume he knows what's wrong and discover that his clairvoyant antenna is kaput. Let the blame rip and duck when his arsenal is launched.

Why do we do this? The short answer is that emotions take charge and fool us. In the heat of the moment they guide us to behaviors that thwart us from getting what we really want. For example, you're angry for being blamed by your boyfriend for losing tickets to a play. You know you didn't, and it can only be him who either lost or misplaced them, yet in his eyes you did it because you are "always losing things."

This is infuriating and you want to tell him in no uncertain terms that you are very angry for being blamed for something you didn't do. So you call him a moron, among other colorful epithets. But another feeling, one more vital, is your desire for fairness. You want him to recognize that he's responsible for the missing tickets, not you, for crying out loud. Curse him out and I'd say you have a better chance of making ice cream in hell than having him acknowledge that. When you engage in a verbal attack, *your most essential desire is not going to be satisfied. You will guarantee the opposite outcome.*

There is a plethora of ways communication can be decimated as temperatures rise. We will examine a number of them. This will provide you with an awareness that will help you avoid them or desist if you find yourself in the midst of one.

Man Talk: The Gay Couple's Communication Guide
© 2007 by The Haworth Press, Inc. All rights reserved.
doi:10.1300/5527_04

Yelling

This is a common and almost knee-jerk reaction for many. Something is said that is not appreciated and the reaction is a rise in decibels. Watch any talking head show and volume often correlates with the degree of disagreement. These shows become comical when numerous guests try to out-shout one another. The aim is get their respective points across. The result: noise.

Shouting is a form of visceral expression. Saying it loud says you're serious. It says you're angry. And it can stop dead what is bothering you. For example, your lover tells you to take out the dog while you're watching television. You shout, "Shut the fuck up" and he does.

But there's a price to pay. You get to watch your program but you have disrespected your lover. What feelings have been induced in him? Perhaps fear in the moment followed by considerable anger. What effect will that have on your peace tomorrow, in an hour, the next time you're watching a show you enjoy?

Shouting has many other negative effects. It may *not* quiet your lover but induce him, instead, to bark back. This can quickly escalate into a shouting match that will leave both of you exhausted, angry, and discontented. Shouting tends to make you angrier. While you may think it's a way to let off steam, it does no such thing. It actually aggravates the irritation, making it increasingly difficult to cool down the longer you're yelling. As you shout you are more likely to say things that you will regret later on. There are some things we say that cannot be retracted no mater how sorry we are or how much we didn't mean it.

> When I yell, I find myself hurting the other person . . . I never found that yelling resolves anything . . . you just say things you don't really mean . . .
>
> Diego, 28, customer service representative,
> Tucson, Arizona

Although yelling is not physical violence, it can lead to it. As you shout and escalate your anger, your sense of omnipotence increases while your judgment and control are likely to decrease. If both of you are escalating, the chance of a physical confrontation increases.

Screaming does nothing to resolve differences. It only creates new problems.

Global Personality Assassination

Being human means we all think and behave in ways that are contemptible at times. Rarely, however, does this describe the total sum of who we are. Your lover may consider himself first more often than you appreciate, and perhaps he is insensitive to your needs much too often. These issues need to be addressed. But if you call him a *"selfish bastard who always thinks only about himself"* you've transformed a description of some of his behavior into a global characterization of his person.

There are two major problems with this. First, such a statement is erroneous. "Thinks *only* about himself *always*" is implausible. It's a nonreality that serves no function other than to create more nonrealities. He's likely to respond with an equally absurd depiction of your person. The other problem is that it's an exercise in absurdity. If he were actually an intrinsically selfish bastard, what's there to argue about? Your only choice would be to either accept him or leave him. Should he have any desire to make changes, you've already told him that you don't believe he can. Your statement has foreclosed the possibility of a change that could bring satisfaction to *you.*

> . . . it forces me into a defensive position, which forces me to be more angry, which forces me to probably explode a little. It stops communication.
>
> Simon, 34, attorney
> Madison, Wisconsin

You may think to yourself that you *know* he's not *always* selfish, but you said it only because you were angry. You didn't really mean it. That's swell, but you haven't communicated that. Your lover doesn't hear what you really mean; he hears what you say. Words are powerful and can be injurious.

Be judicious with the terms always, totally, never, all the time, continuously forever, permanently, completely, entirely, and so forth, particularly in the heat of a disagreement. These words fuel conflict and solve nothing.

Passive-Aggressive Behavior

> Jack did not want to go to dinner when his boyfriend, Allen, called him at his office at two o'clock in the afternoon. Jack was having a very busy day and he would rather kick back at home alone that evening, but he felt uncomfortable saying this to Allen and readily agreed. As five o'clock approached he was feeling very tired and increasingly resentful that Allen was "making" him go to dinner.
>
> They met at McCormick and Schmick, at six p.m., a high-end restaurant in downtown Los Angeles. Normally very talkative, and knowing that Allen loved to converse with him, Jack ate in relative silence. Allen asked him repeatedly if anything was wrong, and Jack said again and again that everything was fine. He kept chewing and Allen kept wondering.
>
> A good time was had by no one, and as they left, Allen was at a loss as to what was amiss. *What the hell is wrong?* he thought. *Was it something I said? Was it that sarcastic remark I made last week about his brother? Did I smell bad?* His thoughts raced as he drove along highway 110 to his home in Pasadena. Jack drove west to Beverly Hills, angry but feeling vindicated. *He should know better than to make me go out on a week night. I guess he's learned his lesson,* he thought.

Passive-aggressive behavior means expressing aggression indirectly. It is one of the most effective ways to destroy communication.

People who are uncomfortable communicating their needs openly resort to this behavior. Beneath the discomfort are a number of problems including fear of conflict, difficulty with self-legitimization of one's needs, a desire to keep others "happy," a dearth of communication skills, or some combination of all of the above. Low self-esteem, in my experience, is always part of the equation. I've never met anyone comfortable in his own skin who couldn't openly express his needs and protect his boundaries.

The example with Jack and Allen shows an externalization of responsibility. It's not Jack's avoidance of saying "no," in his view, that is responsible for going out when he doesn't want to. Allen should know better and shouldn't force him!

People who are passive aggressive tend to be quite angry. That's why it's called passive *aggressive*. They are aware, at least on some level of their needs, but feel at a loss to procure them. Instead of trying to figure out how to change that, they blame others for making their lives miserable, which is a majestic road to nowhere.

Their needs don't just remain quiet but are expressed in a round-about way that in effect is expressing anger. In the previous example, Jack knew he was behaving differently and that this would impact Allen. His refusal to acknowledge that something was wrong just added to his punishment of Allen, but he wasn't expressing his needs. Allen didn't have a clue, nor should he have had, about what was bothering Jack.

The recipient of passive-aggressive behavior is powerless to do anything. He cannot read his boyfriend's mind, and it's certainly not his job to extricate information that his boyfriend should be revealing. Resolving conflicts are difficult enough. Struggling to identify the conflict adds barriers to communication that are entirely unnecessary.

Those who have problems expressing their needs directly should look at the reasons behind that and take action. Sometimes an assertiveness training group can be helpful. Sometimes therapy is requisite. If you are the partner of someone who has been passive aggressive and he makes an attempt to express his needs directly, I would be very supportive. It doesn't mean you have to agree with what he says. But the act of saying it directly is the beginning of a potential resolution to a problem, and should be encouraged. Healthy communication in a relationship cannot coexist with passive aggressive behavior.

Kicking the Dog (or Your Boyfriend)

Life in the twenty-first century can be maddening at times. Stress is in our lifeblood, and it's often a challenge to remain calm and rational. But this never gives you license to take your unhappiness out on your lover.

As we get comfortable with the person we love, he becomes privy to our less-than-attractive sides. That is normal and inevitable. You may say things to him that you wouldn't say to a stranger. You are more relaxed with him and don't have to watch your every word. You may put your foot in your mouth on occasion and no significant negative consequences will occur. That is very different from feeling that if the world hasn't been nice to you, you can be nasty to him.

Most of us do not have the conscious thought that "I had a bad day today so I'll go home and attack my boyfriend." More likely the anger is displaced in a way that may appear reasonable at first glance. The perpetrator may not even realize that he's shifting his focus. The end result, nevertheless, is the creation of an issue out of nothing, or the amplification of a small problem into a full-scale crisis. Sometimes it results in an emotional explosion that can be highly damaging to the relationship.

Example 1: Amplification of a Mini Problem

Jessie and Myron live together in Boston, Massachusetts. They have been together for six years and always have had somewhat of a struggle over keeping their large house clean. Neither one of them could win the Good Housekeeping Seal of Cleanliness. On one particular Sunday morning in late December, Myron woke up with a raging sinus headache. He had some work to complete on his computer before Monday and loathed the task, particularly because he was feeling so ill. But the report was already overdue and he could not postpone it any longer. En route to his home office on the first floor, he noticed that the dishes hadn't been done from the previous night. He had cooked so it was Jessie's job to do the dishes. He saw red.

He yelled "Jessie, could you come downstairs . . . now?"

Jessie appeared.

JESSIE: What's up?

MYRON: What happened with these dishes?

JESSIE: Oh sorry . . . I forgot. I fell asleep.

MYRON: Isn't it your responsibility to do the dishes when I cook? If you didn't want to wash five dishes, then at least throw them in the dishwasher. You're not supposed to leave them out.

JESSIE: You're right. I'm sorry.

MYRON: *No you're not.* You do this all the time. Now we're going to have ants. I work my ass off to pay the mortgage and you shit up this house.

JESSIE: I pay half of the mortgage. What are you talking about?

MYRON: You are irresponsible. I take care of this house. If I don't do it, it doesn't get done.

JESSIE. Myron, I made a mistake. I'm sorry. I'll do the dishes now.

MYRON: Excuses, excuses. Always an excuse for everything. You just don't care.

JESSIE: Wait a minute. That is not true. I AM SORRY. Why are you making such a big deal out of this? What do you want?

MYRON: I want you to be responsible.

JESSIE: Myron, go to hell. You can take the dishes; the whole damn set, and shove them up your stupid ass. I'm going to Mary's house. You're a maniac and I can't deal with this now.

Example 2: Nonissue

Dimitri is a risk manager in a Denver hospital. He had experienced a grueling day dealing with the son and daughter of a woman who died after a fall while being assisted out of bed by a nurse. They were threatening to sue. He had been in back-to-back meetings throughout the day with the staff on the unit at the time of the incident, and attorneys for the hospital. He hadn't eaten since breakfast and was feeling ill. To make matters worse his commute home had been a nightmare. Snow had blanketed the city and his thirty-minute drive took two hours. He was exhausted. When he walked into the house, his lover Max was just finishing a telephone conversation. When he hung up, the following conversation ensued.

DIMITRI: Whom were you just talking to?

MAX: No hello?

DIMITRI: Whom were you just talking to?

MAX: It was Jane. She said hello.

DIMITRI: I don't like her.

MAX: Really? That's news to me. Since when don't you like her?

DIMITRI: Since now.

MAX: Why?

DIMITRI: 'Cause I don't like her. Isn't that good enough? Do I have to justify everything in our relationship?

MAX: Looks like someone had a bad day. Why are you all of a sudden attacking Jane?

DIMITRI: Keep my day out of this.

MAX: Look, you're way, way late. It was a lousy drive with the snow?

DIMITRI: Keep my fucking commute out of this! Listen, Max, I hate your damn friend Jane.

MAX: You hate her? What is going on? We've always had fun together with her. What's this all about? I never had any inkling that she made you uncomfortable.

DIMITRI: I didn't say she makes me uncomfortable. I just don't like her. She's a big mouth and she's always in our business. She also calls too much.

MAX: Wow . . . when did this start? You never told me before that you felt this way.

DIMITRI: Well, I'm telling you know. I don't like that cackling fat slut. Next time she calls I'm hanging up on her.

MAX: Have you been drinking?

Example 3: Confusing the Match with the Dynamite

· Sometimes you can be so stressed and overwhelmed that your lover commits the crime of breathing in your presence and you commence war. In a situation like this, you are so geared up that it will take very, very little to set you off.

Jonathan, a twenty-eight-year-old bookstore clerk and student living in Seattle, was having trouble paying his bills. All at once he seemed to be drowning in debt. An unexpected problem with his car cost him $800. The new school year was beginning and he had to buy books. His landlord raised the rent. To make matters worse, his boss had just informed him that she would have to cut back his hours because the store wasn't doing well.

Jonathan was very worried and stayed up more than one night trying to figure out how to get out of the mess. He did not tell his boyfriend, Earl, what was going on because he was embarrassed.

He was feeling deprived and particularly upset one morning when the bank called, asking him about his car payment. He was behind a month and frankly didn't know how he could continue to both pay for his car and eat. And he needed his car to get to work and school.

That evening (which was a Friday night) Earl said that he wanted to go with him to a club that had just opened. When Jonathan suggested that they just hang out at his place, Earl was disappointed. Rather nonchalantly he said, "You don't seem to be much fun anymore."

That caused an explosion that rattled the Seattle Space Needle!

Jonathan tore into Earl, accusing him of not caring about him, of being superficial and only wanting a good time. The decibels kept rising as Jonathan declared what a good-for-nothing Earl was and that he only wanted his blood, like everyone else.

"Hey . . . I didn't mean anything by that . . . what's going on?" Earl asked.

"Get out of my house," Jonathan answered.

At a total loss about what was happening, he pleaded with Jonathan to tell him what was going on.

"Get out of my house or I'll kick your ass in," he responded.

Earl left confused, worried, and angry.

Jonathan had finally reached the end of the line. "How dare the whole world screw me over" was the overriding message in his tirade. However, a gathering of unfortunate events had caused his dismay, not Earl. Earl's not particularly intelligent comment was a spark flickering near an unknown pile of dynamite. Taking out his pent-up emotions on Earl gave Jonathan a momentary sense of relief at the cost of alienating Earl and making his situation even more problematic.

Jonathan would have been better served had he told Earl what was going on. It's likely Earl would have never made that comment knowing Jonathan's situation. Regardless, Jonathan's distress derived from his state of affairs, not anything Earl could say or not say. Always keep this is in mind if you feel you're about to explode on your lover. Is he really the dynamite (what has really been bothering you) or an unwitting spark that can be extinguished before you create further unhappiness for yourself (and him)?

When Solution Isn't the Goal

PHILLIP: We overdrew the joint account because you insisted on buying those plants.

DENNIS: You're right.

PHILLIP: I'm not paying the overdraft penalty.

DENNIS: I don't expect you to. I will.

PHILLIP: You should never have insisted on buying those plants.

DENNIS: You're right. I didn't balance the checkbook. I made a mistake. I was wrong.

PHILLIP: Yeah, you were too in love with those plants.

DENNIS: I'm sorry. It was an oversight. It's my fault. I will pay the penalty fee.

PHILLIP: That was very stupid Dennis. You should know what's in the account first.

DENNIS: For Christ sakes, Phillip, would you give this a rest? I made a mistake, I'm sorry, and I will pay the fee. Now let it go.

PHILLIP: Why should I? You're an idiot. I'm mad at you.

Sometimes a problem is clear and the guilty party takes full responsibility, yet the fight continues. Why?

Some folks are invested in the process of uncovering blame and establishing their righteousness. The aim is to achieve both triumph by showing how the boyfriend screwed up and guilt inducement (That's bad; you're a moron. I would never do that. It shows me who you really are.) for the offense.

None of this can contribute to solving a problem. This is a form of anticommunication, because information isn't shared between two people. Rather, a narcissistic endeavor is undertaken to demonstrate how good one is in contrast to how bad one's partner is.

This points to a problem within the blaming partner. He needs this victory in order to feel better about himself. Of course this will do nothing to enhance his self-esteem and is very likely to cause relationship chaos.

In the example of Phillip and Dennis it's apparent that this argument should have been over before it started. Dennis recognizes his mistake and takes full responsibility for the consequences of his actions, but this does not end it for Phillip because that is not his agenda.

In a situation like this, it's imperative for the blaming partner to hear what is being said and to consider that his agenda is not related to the problem at hand. If you are the partner who is being blamed and you have already taken full responsibility, your job is over. I would suggest not continuing the dialogue because it's a circular process that will only exhaust both of you.

"Winning" and "Losing"

Striving to "win" is an entrenched American value. We are rewarded for being "right," for defeating a competitor, for presenting the better line of reasoning. This does not fare well in a relationship. Love is about intimacy. When you can both understand where each of you are coming from, you foster intimacy. Striving to be right means you are determined to demonstrate that your partner is wrong. This leaves the problem unsolved while eroding closeness.

> . . . it's not always about being right . . . it's about what's right for us and what's right for the relationship . . .
>
> Aidan, 37, physical therapist
> Tampa, Florida

As destructive as striving for "victory" is, it's not easy to leave a lifeblood value at the front door. It takes considerable effort to switch off the competitive determination of the outside world when you deal with your lover.

But you can. It starts by realizing that unlike the outside world, there is no payoff for being right. The cheering audience is only in your head. It also means remembering—even if you have to repeat it to yourself—that this is your lover, not your enemy. You want to love him, not prevail over him. Winning will be a hollow victory.

This doesn't mean you can't put forth your position and point out the logic of the way you see something. It doesn't imply you can't be righteously angry. *But it does mean that your goal is to solve the problem and move on.*

Deciding that this is your goal is requisite. However, communicating that effectively is also imperative. You may want to solve the problem, but without using the appropriate communicative tools, you can easily revert to a blowout. When both of you are irritated, the wrong words or tone can quickly activate the reflexive impulse to win.

In the following vignette, we will see how a problem can degenerate into a win/lose interaction. We will also see how the same issue can be resolved via effective communication.

Quincy and Colin live in Chelsea in New York City. They had planned to see the ten p.m. showing of a movie in an Upper East Side theater. Quincy, as usual, had procrastinated and had left them with little time to get uptown. When they arrived, the movie was already fifteen minutes in progress. They both decided it was too late.

Win/Lose Scenario

COLIN: Thanks for fucking up my evening.

QUINCY: Come on . . . It took forever for the train to come.

COLIN: It took forever for you to get dressed. I told you we were going to miss the movie. This is always the deal with you. I am sick and tired of being late because of you.

QUINCY: I am missing the movie also.

COLIN: You should be missing the movie because you *caused us* to miss it. Don't you complain. You should be apologizing to me for what you did.

QUINCY: Okay . . . [sarcastically] I'm sorry.

COLIN: For crying out loud, you need to admit you are wrong. You need to take responsibility for this bullshit. You are always late; you always screw up stuff for me because you can't be on time.

QUINCY: Fuck you . . . you are late also . . . plenty of times.

COLIN: When, asshole?

QUINCY: Plenty of times. Don't attack me.

COLIN: Why don't you admit that you are wrong, that you ruined this night, that you have an *inability* to be on time?

QUINCY: I'm going. You can stand here and talk to yourself.

Problem-Solving Scenario

COLIN: I'm really upset that we are missing this movie.

QUINCY: Me too.

COLIN. You know, Quincy . . . we needed to leave before nine. I kept telling you we had to get out. And my dear, this isn't the first time this has happened.

QUINCY: I know. I'm a stupid fuck up.

COLIN: No, that's not what I'm saying. I'm saying we need to figure out a way so this doesn't keep happening.

QUINCY: Do you have any suggestions?

COLIN: You need to take a serious look at how you are very often late and do something about it. I'll be honest . . . especially when I'm with you. If you want to be late your own, that's your business.

QUINCY: Yup.

COLIN: So what do you want to do about this?

QUINCY: I think it's obvious. I really have to leave more time to get to places. I think when I'm getting ready that I sort of fall into this unrealistic appraisal until it hits me how late I'm running.

COLIN: Could I make a suggestion?

QUINCY: Sure.

COLIN: Next time we have to go somewhere, let me decide when we have to leave. Even if you think it's unnecessarily early, let me make that decision.

QUINCY. That sounds fair.

COLIN: Which means that if we have to get out by nine and your hair is not right or whatever, we still leave. Unless you can seriously commit to that, nothing is going to improve.

QUINCY: I see that. There has to be a real change, not just talking about it. I'll let you decide the time and I will follow through. Hair, face, or whatever. Ready or not.

COLIN: That sounds great.

QUINCY: Now let me get you a drink.

COLIN: And a pizza.

QUINCY: You can kiss my butt (laughing).

Everything Including the Kitchen Sink

Bringing up issues from the past is a way to throw someone off the scent of what is really going on in the present.

Brian Wolfe, MFT
formerly in private practice, San Francisco, CA
(now living in New Zealand)

Disagreements over one issue is adequately challenging for any-one. When you bring up multiple issues, especially problems from the past, you're headed for a brawl that will lead nowhere. This oc-curs with old angers and conflicts that never reached closure. The current anger activates the old sleeping dogs and they come out at-tacking for ancient wrongs.

Dredging up old sins is attack ammunition; it can't co-exist with rational dialogue. You may consciously think *Let me get this all on the table now so we can straighten this out* but that is not the real ob-jective. The intention is to pounce, not come to any resolution, and your lover will know it. His likely reactions will be (1) dredging up your ten-year-old sins; (2) going on the defensive about what he did (wasn't so bad; it didn't really happen the way you remember it; you're lying); (3) ignoring you. You both will wind up angrier at each other.

Even if there was a magical way to somehow remove the attack component, multiple, current, and ancient alleged misdeeds cannot be resolved when they are thrown together. Too much material, too many complicated feelings, and two much raw emotion are involved to allow any constructive focus.

No matter how angry you are, no matter how you can see that the wrong perpetrated on you this time is similar to all those other bad things he did to you, *cease and desist!* If you want to solve what is happening now, stay on topic, focus on what just happened, and look for a way this can be changed. Don't thwart *your own goal.* The rule is only one conflict at a time, and the sooner you can address it, the better. If you have many unresolved concerns, working as a couple with a therapist will probably be necessary to handle those issues at the right pace if there is any hope of resolution.

Taking Forever to Let Go

A relationship of significant duration will ultimately result in mis-takes that hurt. You say or do something without thinking. You're in-sensitive, you forget, or purposely commit a malicious act.

Forgiveness is generally a choice, but not always. Some mistakes can exceed your boundary of exoneration. For example, you discover that your lover has been having a long-term clandestine affair. As much as you would like to forgive, you are not *able* to do so. In this situation there's few options. Staying healthy means you can't be with this man any longer. Inability to forgive and having a viable relationship are mutually exclusive.

But many mistakes don't reach this level. They cause hurt but are relatively benign and we eventually get over them. We *are able* to choose to let go and move on. We can also choose how long that will take.

Some folks hold on to hurt because they find it daunting to directly communicate how bad they feel. The "Sitting Bull method" feels easier. Such a person doesn't have to deal with the messy stuff of conflict. He simply remains stone faced and his message, he believes, will get across. He also wants to make his lover pay for what he has done. Staying pissy and irritated and blaming delivers punishment. After enough contrition by his lover, after enough apologies, after perhaps enough days, he slowly lets go of the hurt. This is not beneficial to anyone. Not letting go increases anger for both men, erodes communication, and begets other problems.

Holding on and ruminating about what he did to you will have a tendency to make you angrier. Inside the walls of your skull there is no chance for a better understanding or for hearing that your lover is sorry. You simply get a rerun of a lousy movie that has upset you and will re-antagonize you. Furthermore, rumination has a way of exaggerating the actual situation. This is similar to anxious rumination in which the scenes in your mind are much more frightening than the actual event or what will come to pass. In effect the Sitting-Bull method solves nothing, but tends to cause reinjury and additional uneasiness.

Holding on will upset your lover. Whether or not he agrees that he has done anything wrong, he is deprived of the opportunity to negotiate with you. He is forced to remain in a holding pattern while he experiences the punishment of your wrath. This is likely to incite his anger. Ironically, he may retreat from acknowledging that he made a mistake and go on the attack. Now you've succeeded in *not* addressing the first problem and creating a second one.

Holding on takes away precious time. Life is complicated and difficult enough, and the natural order of things creates a full supply of conflicts in the best of relationships. If you hold onto anger you may find little time to do anything else. As you finally resolve one problem, another one arrives. Furthermore, the almost continuous feeling of anger has a way to "prime" your emotional system into lowering your threshold for anger. This can create a destructive cycle in which both of you are habitually in conflict.

Learning to let go means recognizing that you have a choice to do this. Holding on signifies avoidance of the work of problem solving, and punishment of your lover in a passive-aggressive manner.

> . . . it's easier to be angry than to deal with any other kind of emotion. It sort of shields you from having to deal with more vulnerable kinds of feelings . . . a person who does that has a need to really hold off intimacy.
>
> Betty Berzon, PhD
> private practice
> Los Angeles, California

Believing "I just can't get over this now," is a cop out. Getting over it begins by discussing how you are feeling and relinquishing the wish to punish.

Disrespect

Those of us with even half-baked self-esteem require respect. We count on being heard, taken seriously, told the truth, having our feelings considered, and being valued as human beings. When this treatment is not forthcoming from others, we cannot continue a relationship with such folks. Disrespect communicates to the recipient that he doesn't matter, that he can be treated with contempt, and that he doesn't deserve better. It's the antithesis of intimacy. Suffice it to say that you and your lover need to respect one another.

Ironically, sometimes disrespect is related to the comfort of a relationship. We begin to take a boyfriend for granted, and may be disrespectful without even realizing it. Saying "shut up" or walking away while he's talking may not seem like a big deal to you. But consider this: Did you behave that way when you first met? Probably not, because it would eat away at the relationship you were creating. That is no less true in your current situation. Love needs continuous support, and when you are disrespectful you erode the sustenance you both need. Don't let the comfort of your longevity fool you into the false belief that disrespect is part of being together or that it can't tear the two of you apart.

Another, even more critical issue, is when lovers build up resentment over time and then act it out via disrespect. It becomes a form of familiar behavior that is justified by the resentment. For example, you stay out late, don't call, and thus cause him to worry. Rationalization: You are fed up with his control and don't think you need to report to him. Next example: You refuse him the opportunity to listen when he wants to speak. Rationalization: He has nothing worthwhile to say. Another example: You decide to be "funny" when out with friends and reveal a secret that humiliates him. Rationalization: What's the problem, you ask yourself? Can't he take a joke?

Relationship and disrespect are mutually exclusive. This must be changed if you want a relationship that will enhance rather than detract from your life. If you are the recipient of disrespect, nothing you do or don't do merits this. It's a relationship and self-esteem killer. Don't stand for it.

Threatening to Break Up

> I make it a rule with couples that they're not allowed to say "I'm going to break up with you" in this room [her office] and that they take a vow that they won't say that outside this room unless they've got their bags packed and they're in the car.
>
> Betty Berzon, PhD
> private practice
> Los Angeles, California

These are words of war and you should think long and hard before you say them. My rule parallels that of Dr. Berzon's: Don't declare you intend to break up unless you have decided to do it. In that case it will not be a threat but rather a statement of fact. And I have a second rule. Don't ever utter those words in the heat of conflict.

Breaking up can be an appropriate decision. It's suitable when it's arrived at after careful, sober consideration and a realization that your relationship is no longer viable. This is *not* what I'm referring to here.

Unfortunately, "let's break up" is a mantra that is used by many as soon as any discomfort is experienced. "I'm tired of you telling me what to do. I'm out of here." "How dare you call me that? We're finished." "You don't understand me. I need a boyfriend who does. I'm leaving you, Tommy."

For a gay couple the threat of breaking up is one of the most destructive acts to both the relationship and communication. The belief that gay relationships never last is vintage homophobia that has both a long history in our community and one that many gay folks struggle with today. The heart of this thinking, as politically incorrect as this may sound, is the belief that the relationship is defective from the start, that the people in it are defective, and therefore no long-term relationship is really possible. Most gay men, in my view, do not consciously articulate nor believe this position and could rightfully point to the homophobic bias behind this. But countless messages over a lifetime impact us despite the conscious part of our minds that knows such reasoning is erroneous. Furthermore, we're all familiar with couples who have not made it. So the cloud of breaking up becomes a kind of dark expectation that lives with you everyday of your relationship life. Then the minute something goes wrong, the threat is articulated. I want you to hear loud and clear that this is *very destructive.*

The threat brings to life the belief that lingered in the back of your mind. In that instant the internal thought becomes external reality. Then the ground you're standing on begins to crumble. The fear was always there but threatening you brings it to a whole new level. It confirms that indeed these relationships don't last and here goes mine.

Intimacy is about deep trust, about safety and security, about knowing you can count on this person. When he's threatening to leave you, (even when he doesn't) that comfort is decimated. It's not difficult to see how intimacy goes out with this bathwater. How can you rest in the comfort of your love when at any time he can just tell you that it's all over, that he will no longer be there, that all you know will be changed in a second? The answer is that you will not rest. Intimacy will decrease as your walls of defense are fortified.

Some people repeatedly threaten to leave whenever conflict arises. Although the partner may begin to see this as an empty threat, it still poses a danger to the stability of the relationship. It communicates the message "don't count on this relationship."

Threatening to break up stops communication dead. Healthy communication means that you feel safe to express what you feel in an effort to find a solution. If you are going to be threatened with breaking up, you will not be open and communication will not occur. Threatening to break up may have an unintended effect: Your lover just may take you up on it. Realizing that you didn't really mean it may not be able to stop the forces you have unleashed.

Why Do We Do It?

The threat of a breakup can be powerful ammunition. This can work to startle your lover and make him retreat from an aggressive stance. He may pull back from letting you have it and become subservient as he fears your abandonment. This reverses the power dynamic at once. You are no longer under attack but in charge. This instant change is seducing and becomes your MO whenever you feel threatened.

Breaking up signifies release from the complexities of a relationship. All the aggravation and high maintenance and confused feelings disappear at once if he is no longer in your life. So the statement becomes a kind of fantasy vacation from the turmoil you're in at the moment. You don't actually have to break up. Just saying it reminds you that you have the option of escape, which can reduce your feeling of being trapped.

Still another reason for threatening to break up is that breaking up is your expectation and your "programmed" response. The thought goes like this: "Well, I really knew this was going to happen. Here it is [the "impossible" problems I am having with him] so I'll do what I know how to do, what I have done before, and what I have expected would be necessary all along." In this scenario you may actually leave.

By becoming aware of these forces right now as you're reading this book and (I assume) not in the middle of a fight with him, you may prevent yourself from uttering those words. Hopefully, he's doing the same.

Continuous Criticism

None of us live in a nonjudgmental bubble. When your boyfriend does something stupid, you're probably going to tell him about it. Criticism can even be helpful. If his clothes don't match before you leave for a party, you may save him from embarrassment by sharing your critique of his appearance.

But you're not his mother and it's not your role to teach him right from wrong. If that's what occurring, you're changing your equal relationship between two equal adults to an unequal one between a par-

ent and child. He will resent that and you will too. Parenting is drain-
ing and being treated like a child is infuriating. You therefore need to
ask yourself if criticism is defining your relationship rather than being an occasional expression of concern and/or irritation.

An atmosphere of continuous criticism dominates the lives of
some couples. Discussion is about "what you did wrong" and "why
you should do it my way—the right way." It may not be verbalized
exactly like that, but that's exactly what's being conveyed. No one is
going to honestly communicate what he thinks and feels if there is a
virtual guarantee that it will cause disapproval. Your lover will come
to view you as a nagging, hypercritical parent, not a supportive lover.

Continuous criticism poisons the quality of your time together.
Rather than an oasis of calm from a harried world, your relationship
becomes a place of intense stress. The outside world may look more
inviting. That's a bad sign. Real feelings will be hidden. He will edit
and sanitize his account of what he does out of fear you'll tell him he
did it wrong. Your counsel won't be sought when he's frightened or
depressed or has to make an important decision. You can truly be shut
out of his life.

There's a good chance your criticism comes from a place of wanting to help, not hurt. You've made the mistakes he's about to make or
made and want to save him from further damage. Give that a rest. You
may actually be right but continuously criticizing him will not help.
Repeat. *It will not help.* If you can really accept this, you should be
able to resist the temptation to criticize. Your laudable goal of wanting to help will not be realized and you will only make matters worse.
The best way to be there for him is to listen first and advise if he invites you to do so. Advice can be imparted without the implication or
statement that he's an idiot if he doesn't take it.

Mind Reading

I don't know if you have psychic abilities, but as a therapist I would
tell you that there are better ways to get through to your boyfriend.
One way is to tell him what you need. This is easier said than done.
You may not know what you need. You may be experiencing a conun-
drum of complex emotions that are difficult to verbalize. You may not
trust his response. Perhaps, you think, he'll laugh in your face. So the
easier way is do nothing and assume that he should know, and that he

should react accordingly to what you're thinking and feeling. And when he doesn't, get angry with him.

Hmm . . . I think this is questionable reasoning. Being angry is easier than the messy stuff of direct communication. The problem is that it will get you nowhere. Mind reading doesn't exist and it's foolhardy to be angry with him when he can't do the impossible. While you're likely to be more in tuned with each other as you relationship grows through time, this is not a viable means to get your point across. The best way is to simply say what you think and feel as best you can. In an atmosphere where criticism is minimal, this will involve minimal emotional risk.

Negative Assumptions and Expectations

All of us develop beliefs about our partners based on our experiences with them. For example, if you believe he's reliable (because he has been) you'll assume that he will be there at the airport to meet you if he told you he would. Negative experiences result in negative expectations; they work essentially the same way, with one difference: Negative predictions can obstruct discussion of a problem, erode intimacy, and foreclose the possibility of change.

Francis and Howard are a couple living together in Boston for the past two years. Francis has been undependable a couple of times in different situations. They have never openly addressed the issue. Howard has grown frustrated and angry and dismisses any possibility that Francis might change. In the following vignette, Howard is in Los Angeles for a business trip and will be returning to Boston on the following day. He is speaking on the phone, to Francis who is in Boston.

FRANCIS: What time are you arriving at Logan tomorrow? I'll pick you up.

HOWARD: No, thank you. . . . I remember the last time . . . Don't worry about it. . . . I'll take a cab.

FRANCIS: I know I have disappointed you before, more than once. But I will definitely be there tomorrow.

HOWARD: Much, much more than once! *Sure* you'll be there. *So will dead Grandma Helen.*

FRANCIS: Come on, Howie . . . I mean it.

HOWARD: No. Don't bother. I'm not going to sit there like a fool waiting for you. A cab will be just fine. I'll see you when I get home.

FRANCIS: But Howard, I really want to do this for—

HOWARD: (interrupting) I said no. *No.* I'll see you when I get home. I'm not talking about this anymore.

What's wrong with this? Francis has a history of not always show-ing up when he says he will, he's aware of this, and is saying that he's trying to do something about it. (We don't know if he's sincere, or even if he is, if he will actually follow through.) Howard's negative expectation, while certainly justified, *forecloses* the possibility of re-solving this problem if he permits his expectation to control his be-havior.

Francis's less than adult behavior is certainly not Howard's re-sponsibility. Furthermore, it's not easy for Howard to believe that Francis will change when he has burned him repeatedly. Negative ex-pectations, like positive expectations, seem very natural because our expectations are what we have experienced and know to be true. But what may seem to be absolute truth is not necessarily so.

Should Howard accept Francis's offer and Francis doesn't come through again, Howard will be considerably disappointed. But in-stead of concluding that before it happens, I'd suggest that Howard use this as an opportunity to express to Francis his frustration and de-sire for real change.

I recognize that a long-distance telephone call is not the best means to address a serious issue. But since it involves meeting Howard at the airport on the following day, Howard would need to begin the dia-logue then. Of course, more discussion will be required once they are together. Howard could say the following on the phone:

"Francis, I would love for you to pick me up and I appreciate the gesture, but you often don't show up when you say you will. That bothers me and it will really hurt if I come off that airplane tomorrow expecting you to be there and you aren't. So let's talk about this. What's going on that causes you to flake out so often? Is something going to be different tomorrow? Tell me, please. I want more than good intentions. If you say you're going to be there, I want to know just how you're going to accomplish it. I'm open to hearing what you have to say."

There is no guarantee that Francis will engage in this discussion. He may even respond with "Go to hell. I'm trying do you a favor and you're attacking me." In that case, some cab driver is certainly getting a fare from Howard. But perhaps Francis will be open to addressing the issue. Maybe he really will be there when the plane lands. Why pass over that potential opportunity? Without challenging the expectation, there *is a guarantee* of diminished communication and an increased likelihood that nothing will change.

Before You Go to Work Bombs

Important issues should be brought up only when there is adequate time and the appropriate setting to accommodate them. Major issues engender emotional reactions, and to trigger them and leave your boyfriend hanging is more than unfair. It can create anxiety and resentment that will affect how the issue will eventually be dealt with. You may first have to handle the fallout of poor timing before you can even approach the original issue.

What constitutes a significant issue is anything that will have an important impact on both of you. It's a judgment call, but some unambiguous examples include:

- Bringing up any major change in your relationship, especially a desire to separate or break up.
- Deciding to leave your job, having been fired, or any major financial change.
- Wanting to relocate to another city.
- Announcing that you have or may have a serious health problem.

Dropping a bomb and walking away creates a power disparity. You've been aware of what's going on. He didn't know anything about it. He's being confronted with momentous change and has to deal with it by himself. He also needs to concentrate on his job or whatever else he's doing that day. Preoccupation with what you told him will interfere with that. He may be overcome with anxiety that could have been avoided or at least minimized had he had an opportunity to talk about it with you.

Why do we do this to the person we love? Sometimes we have no mal intent and just don't realize the inappropriateness of the timing. By being sensitive to the effect on him, you'll be able to avoid this mistake.

Another reason is the "dumping and running" phenomenon. This is a classic way to release anxiety destructively. *There, I told him* goes the thought, as you are relieved of the pressure. Since you, or him, or both of you have to rush out the door, there's no time to get into the meat of the matter, which is exactly what you want—to avoid the messy stuff of dealing with the bomb. This is irrational because you must deal with it eventually. Furthermore, if he's been stressed out all day because of this, you're going to have a much larger bomb to diffuse that evening.

Sometimes the reason is to hurt, pure and simple. You're aware of the power differential, you know he's going to stew about the news, and that's exactly what you want. You'll get the adrenalin of being in charge for the moment, but if you also hope to communicate, you'll lose on that score. You'll also prime him to get revenge. In other words, this will come back to bite you in the ass.

So what is the right time and place to discuss matters like this? A suitable occasion requires, foremost, adequate time. Don't start a serious discussion when you know you will have to keep an appointment later on. Sometimes an important issue will take a lot longer than you think, and you don't want to be pressured to finish prematurely. An appropriate time also means that neither of you is in a bad mood where anything said could easily commence an argument. The topic you will be addressing may be upsetting enough, so beginning it when there's stress in the air is only asking for trouble.

It's also imperative to do this in a comfortable, private environment. Don't be interrupted with phone calls, pagers, or anything else. Avoid the use of chemicals. Having a drink (or many) may seem helpful if you anxiety is high. It will have the opposite effect, however. Drinking and other chemicals alter your judgment and can disinhibit your emotions. Having a reasonable discussion under those conditions is impossible.

Threatening or Doing Violence

Physical violence or the possibility of violence ends communication. Communication is about connecting with your partner. You can connect only when you feel comfortable expressing what you think and feel. That is out of the question if there's any risk that you can be physically hurt.

Threats of violence, whether or not they are carried out, have the same deleterious effect on communication. Domestic violence is complex and beyond the scope of this book to address in any detail. It is an exceedingly serious problem that needs professional intervention immediately. Violence is *never* a normal part of the stress and work of being in a relationship. It cannot be worked out between just the two of you. An outsider, a professional who knows what he or she is doing, needs to be involved.

The main theme of this book, learning better methods of communication, cannot be applied when violence is in the picture. Violence guarantees no limits. Put simply, he could maim or kill you. It makes no sense to try to improve communication when saying the wrong word could land you in the hospital.

Violence must end before other aspects of your relationship can improve. Quite frankly, your relationship may have run its course if physical aggression has occurred. Violence crosses a line, a point of possible no return because among other evils, trust may be irrevocably shattered.

I want to repeat that it is imperative that you seek professional help. Even the decision to leave must be discussed with a professional because the act of leaving could result in danger. If you contact a mental health facility, ask if they have staff who have training in gay male domestic violence. If not, ask for a reference to a person or facility that can provide such expertise. If you have a LGBT community organization in your area, ask them.

Avoidance

Evasion makes communication progressively more difficult because the more you avoid, the more you build the monster. If you are not satisfied sexually and say nothing, over time the subject becomes even more taboo. Your mind perceives evidence that this is not talked about by your history of avoidance. Circular reasoning yes, but unfortunately it works. Furthermore, unaddressed relationship problems always get worse.

In my experience there are a number of topics that are particularly difficult for gay couples to meet head-on. In the next chapter we tackle these subjects, learn how to cope with the fears they bring, and thus create a better understanding between you and your partner.

Chapter 4

Communication Minefields: The Seven Deadly Topics Gay Men Won't Talk About

...having failed at relationships before, I'm more worried about the un-said things than about the said things.

Christian, 36, real estate agent
Miami Beach, Florida

Intimacy means connection but it doesn't mean unrestricted access. All of us have private thoughts and feelings we don't share. This makes sense because it delineates our individuality. If you felt you had to share every thought and emotion with your boyfriend, you'd no longer feel like a separate person. Furthermore, your boyfriend wouldn't want this. Unrestricted disclosure is information overload.

This is not the same thing, however, as avoiding difficult relationship issues. For example, you have a monogamous agreement but want to have sex with others. Perhaps you tell yourself that it's your private thought and you don't have to let him know about it. If you do not need to act upon it, if it's simply a passing notion, then it really can stay with you. But if monogamy is no longer acceptable, and you don't address it with him, you are left with two equally bad choices. You either cheat on him or do nothing and become resentful.

Communication minefields are frightening, complex, relationship issues that most couples would rather not have to deal with. I have identified seven of these. They include the following:

1. Your sexual relationship with your boyfriend
2. Sexual interest in others

Man Talk: The Gay Couple's Communication Guide
© 2007 by The Haworth Press, Inc. All rights reserved.
doi:10.1300/5527_05

3. Having an open relationship
4. Money
5. Insecurity about being loved
6. Addiction (chemical and behavioral)
7. Ambivalence about being in your relationship

Minefields

I call them minefields because left to fester they will blow up in your face. I have identified these seven because they represent spheres of conflict for many gay couples. Some may not apply to you or you may have others that are not on the list. I would add them. Whatever your individual situation, communication minefields have common characteristics. We don't like to deal with them and avoiding them makes them worse—much worse. In this chapter we are going to learn how to handle them.

Avoiding Emotional Discomfort

It's imperative to start this journey with exploring and possibly expanding your tolerance for emotional discomfort. Discomfort is not very comfortable! It's not fun and it's not sexy and it's not something a sane person strives for. But many of us confuse emotional uneasiness with "anguish" "torture," and "I can't stand this." Many of us secretly believe that if we can just get it right in life we would avoid almost all unpleasantness.

If you think this way, you're not alone. As a society, we're terribly pain avoidant. Pain is like the devil and we're willing to do almost anything to stay away from it. But life is not only about bliss and pain often brings growth. If you are in an adult relationship and plan to stay in one, discomfort, at times, is part of the package. If you try to avoid it at all costs you will achieve long-term pervasive pain that is much worse than what you avoided. I hate to sound like that guy who sell suits, but *I guarantee it.*

So we start by making peace with pain and accept that when you talk about a weighty topic with your lover, you will experience it. But there is a reward for the effort. *Dealing* with a problem gives you the best shot at resolving it.

Your Sexual Relationship

> . . . people in general in this society have a hard time talking honestly, openly about sex. We're not taught to talk about it; we're taught to just do it.
>
> Betty Berzon, PhD
> private practice
> Los Angeles, California

> . . . the major taboo subject I have experienced from doing couples therapy for years is sex.
>
> Brian Wolfe, MFT
> formerly in private practice, San Francisco, CA
> (now living in New Zealand)

> . . . if he can't quite perform he gets really upset, and I'm afraid that if I bring it up to him and talk to him about it that's going to make him even more anxious.
>
> Harvey, 42, physician
> Cleveland, Ohio

Few topics have more confusing dimensions than sex in American society. If you're a gay man or lesbian you can multiply that perplexity by a thousand.

Sex is filthy and fascinating, everywhere and hidden. It's godly and sinful, pleasurable and wicked, wonderful and abominable, natural and abnormal. There's good sex and bad sex and kinky sex and hot sex and disappointing sex. It can make you happy, miserable, intimate, detached, horny, confused, confident, embarrassed, self-conscious, angry, jealous, excited, and, on occasion, crazy. This in the context of a homophobic society is what you bring to your relationship. No wonder it's difficult to talk about.

Sex, like any other aspect of your relationship, needs attention. Although some couples can pleasure each other with little verbal communication, this doesn't apply to everyone. We also change, and what worked once no longer does. You may be bored with one activity or want to try something new.

Besides the societal backdrop of discomfort with sex, other reasons why couples avoid discussing their sexual relationship include the following.

- Believing sex should come "naturally"
- Believing you will hurt your partner if you tell him you're not satisfied
- Fear that it will lead to outside sex
- Fear it will end your relationship
- Fear it will open up a Pandora's box of difficulties in your relationship
- Believing you don't have the right to "demand" sexual pleasure
- Believing what you want is not "normal"
- Believing you will sound weird
- Believing sex dies after being together long enough, therefore, what's to talk about?
- Believing it will ruin it if you talk about it

Sexual Power

While it's true that a relationship is much more than sex, you can't discount the power of this force. Sexual dissatisfaction and a happy relationship can't co-exist.

Some couples choose to no longer have sex with each other and remain happily together, but these folks usually have some kind of arrangement that involves outside partners. These people are *not* sexually dissatisfied—it's just that the sex is handled outside of the relationship. This is quite different from those who have little or no sexual gratification period. Sexual unhappiness can lead to breaking up. This can be an unfortunate reason to uncouple because you may have been able to change it.

Sexual frustration can also lead to cheating, which of course may decimate your relationship. This *never justifies* cheating but it's an understandable reaction. If you can't get sex at home, and you can't talk about it, it doesn't take a rocket scientist to figure out what may happen next.

How to Talk About Sex

You need to take a critical look at what's stopping you. The power of the previous mentioned reasons will crumble if you put them to the logic test. If you can appreciate that a belief you've held, even for many years, has no basis in logic and therefore reality, its power over you cannot remain.

Sex Should Come Naturally

I'm not sure where this idea originates, possibly from the belief of natural and "unnatural" sex. As gay men, we know how much sense that makes.

Sex is a form of behavior, and behavior, especially this one, is multifaceted. There are endless ways to behave sexually, countless ways to have fun and an equally number of ways to be bored. Sex is appreciably physical, so how your body responds makes a huge difference. Your stamina at age twenty is not the same at sixty. Fucking all night long like the good old days won't be the same if your back is out. Sex also arises from and generates complicated psychological responses that are mysterious as they are continually evolving. Why is spanking your boyfriend's ass a total turn off to you while the guy next door finds this the epitome of his sexual pleasure? (spanking *his* boyfriend, not yours!) Why do gray beards and baldheads turn some men on while others feel they would be sleeping with great grandpa (and don't want to)? And then what happens when all the cards shift? Your boyfriend who never wanted to get fucked all of a sudden wants to do only that. A top transforming into a bottom? Oh my God!

We really don't know why this happens and the why is beside the point anyway. The fact is that this is the way the beast operates. To assume that none of this requires discussion and negotiation, that your sexual pleasure should just come naturally and automatically forever, makes no sense whatsoever.

Talking About Sex Will Ruin It

This is related to the previous issue. Since sex is a natural intuitive phenomenon, somehow discussing it will take away that experience. No evidence supports that theory.

Legitimacy

> . . . It is awkward simply because it's sex. . . . We all feel a little bit of awk-
> wardness when we talk about sex. . . . I grew up in a family where my
> parents said . . . sex shouldn't be something that you enjoy. He comes
> from a family where they don't talk about sex at all.
>
> Danny, 31, teacher
> Austin, Texas

Communicating about what's going on between the two of you begins with making yourself comfortable with your needs.

Despite the sexual openness of many of us in our community, despite the numerous sexual venues and the colorful celebrations of our
sexuality during Gay Pride and other affairs, there's still great ambivalence about legitimacy for needing and seeking and enjoying sex. I
have worked with sexually active gay men who still expressed discomfort over their behavior. I would hear tales of wild sexual esca-
pades that still ended with feelings of "yuck," "I was such a slut,"
"then I had to amble down the walk of shame," "I can't believe I did
that with him."

One technique I would use is to ask them to imagine that they could
never experience sexual satisfaction again. Somehow their equipment
short circuited and they had to spend the next fifty years or so with *no
hope of ever* having an orgasm again. Viewed in this light, the shame
and guilt began to pale as they saw what's really important and how
irrational the other stuff is. Ask yourself this: How could such intense
pleasure between two consenting adults, done safely, ever be a reason
to feel shameful? So what if you fucked four guys in a sex club, or
kissed your boyfriend's ass on the kitchen table, or fantasized about
being raped by nine nasty cops, or licked the boot of some guy in a jock
strap, or fucked with your boyfriend all night as he called you a bitch
in heat? So what? Did you hurt anyone? Does it make you a worse
lawyer or teacher or bus driver? Did you have fun? Would you *desire*
to never be able to do that?

Revisit this idea anytime you feel that your sexuality is embarrassing or not a legitimate need. It can give the self-legitimacy that sex is a
rightful issue to discuss with your boyfriend if you are not satisfied.

Hurting Him

Telling your boyfriend that you are frustrated may initially bruise his feelings. But you are not saying that anything is intrinsically wrong with his sexuality; you are stating that the *sexual relationship between the two of you* is currently on the fritz. This both removes any implication of blame and opens the very real possibility that it can be changed for the better. Telling your boyfriend that you are not happy can be the beginning of making you and perhaps him much more satisfied. Sometimes it takes very little to make it work. For example:

"Rex, I want you to talk dirty to me when we get in bed. Tell me what a bad boy slut motherfucker I have been."

"Andrew, I know you love to suck me. But you do it for a little too long and my then dick starts to feel raw. Could you alternate with kissing me?"

"Jose, wear a jock strap to bed. It will make me crazy."

Now suppose you are Rex, Andrew, or Jose. You may never have talked dirty, you're not accustomed to interrupting your sucking, or you don't own a jock strap. Comply with your boyfriend's requests anyway. The act itself may not turn you on but the change in your boyfriend will gratify you. And what if by chance wearing that article of clothing or talking dirty or giving his dick a rest gives you a charge you didn't know was there? So little to lose (if anything) and so much to gain by willing to be flexible!

Feeling "Weird"

You'd like him to spank you. You want to call him a filthy slut. You want him to play "Pizza Delivery Boy, ringing the doorbell with a pizza, and rape you." You want to suck his foot.

Your excitement is matched only by your embarrassment. You're a freak, you tell yourself, and resolve to forget about your desires. You couldn't tell him you *really wanted that!*

Terms like weird, bizarre, sick, stupid, silly, ridiculous, nuts, and so on have no place in describing safe, consenting sexuality between adults. Why? Because no type of sex is rational. Why then should some forms be okay and others label you a mental case?

There is nothing more normal about putting a dick in your mouth instead of a toe. A man fucking a woman in the vagina in a bed in the "missionary position" (where the hell does that term come from?) makes no more sense than putting a penis in an anus on the floor of your kitchen while your boyfriend is standing on his head. Calling one activity normal and the other crazy is an arbitrary decision that only makes us feel uncomfortable.

Fears of Opening a Pandora's Box

If you have these fears, there may be serious problems in your relationship. Failing to address your sexuality is the last thing you should be doing.

A Pandora's box needs to be pried open fast, because ultimately it's going to explode! Issues must be out in the open if they are to be dealt with. By the time the box explodes, you may be well past the point of talking.

Discussing your sexual relationship can have many positive effects. If so much strife exists between you and him that you no longer feel sexual with each other, discussion can be the first step toward positive change.

As I mentioned earlier, sexual dissatisfaction can lead to cheating. Talking about it may resolve the problem and therefore prevent outside liaisons. It's also true that beginning a discussion may reveal that it is, in fact, too late in the day. This is harsh medicine to swallow, and denial, in the short run, feels better. But if your relationship is really falling apart, it's going to fall apart anyway. It's better to know this sooner rather than later, so that you can avoid the prolongation of misery.

Long Enough Together Means No Sex

Sex does often decrease in intensity and frequency between partners over a long enough period of time. This is not the same as the absence of sex or having no sexual desire. If you have a sexless relationship and are frustrated, telling yourself that this is inevitable is a lie. This is the way it is *for you* which is obviously not okay.

Sometimes sex stops because you are simply bored, and if you can make changes and spice up the experience, that will transform. Gay couples, just like heterosexual ones, let themselves go after they've been together for a long time (gain weight, care about their appearance, etc.), and this impacts sexuality. Telling your boyfriend that his extra twenty pounds is a turnoff is not easy, but keeping it a secret and not touching him is worse. Intense anger can also kill sexuality. Sometimes a therapist is needed to help resolve the conflicts and reintroduce intimacy.

Sexual Interest in Others

When we get together with another person, we want to feel special to that individual. Sexual exclusivity is one way that is achieved. But exclusive sexual behavior is not the same as exclusive sexual thought. The latter is implausible.

Most of us realize that the ability to be attracted to others does not end the moment you have a lover, yet in some relationships there is an unwritten expectation that it does. A man may feel that he is being unfaithful to his beloved if he thinks about, fantasizes, or masturbates about another guy.

It's not necessary or even appropriate to announce to your boyfriend every sexual thought you have about others. But it's important to acknowledge that it exists and to feel free to express your feelings at times. The problem is that outside attraction may appear like a threat to the special place you hold for him. When a relationship is melting down, sexual interest in others, usually of an obsessive nature, *is* one of the signs of impending meltdown. Attraction to others itself, however, is part of hard wiring and has nothing to do with falling out of love. That is what you need to communicate if he's threatened. This is what you need to hear if it's you who is worried.

An example of how this can be achieved is found in the following conversation between Arnold and Joe. Arnold has just commented about a guy they passed in the street and Joe is not amused:

JOE: Why do you have to do that all the time?
ARNOLD: Do what?
JOE: Tell me how you have the hots for everyone?
ARNOLD: Oh, come on . . . that guy was very cute. Don't you have the same. . .?
JOE: Stop it.
ARNOLD: Wait a second . . . you're really upset about this.
JOE: I am.
ARNOLD: Why?
JOE: Because it's not right.
ARNOLD: What is not right?
JOE: Not right telling me how you want to fuck every guy you see.

ARNOLD: I guess I do that too often. But why is it upsetting you? You know I love you and we are monogamous. I am just expressing *feelings*.

JOE: It just seems that your desires for others tells me that I'm not good enough for you . . . that you would rather be with those guys.

ARNOLD: I am not saying that at all. *I love you; you're my boyfriend and you turn me on. I don't want to be with anyone but you.* But I do have sexual feelings and thoughts for others. I mean it's part of being alive. Don't you find other guys attractive?

JOE: Well . . . yeah.

ARNOLD: Do you love me less?

JOE: Of course not.

ARNOLD: Well then. . .?

JOE: I guess I have been a little threatened. Sorry.

ARNOLD: Nothing to be sorry about. Just remember who really matters to me. And I added fuel to the fire by overdoing it.

JOE: So I'm still your special guy?

ARNOLD: What do you think?

JOE: I feel better. But could you just keep it a little more to yourself? You do it too much.

ARNOLD: You're right and I'll cut back . . . somewhat.

JOE: Okay [chuckling]. Thanks, honey.

Open Relationships

In my personal and professional experience, most gay male couples, sooner or later, have to tackle the question of outside sexual experiences. Our community is more tolerant of this than our heterosexual friends, which is both a blessing and a curse. We have potentially more freedom, sexual diversity, sexual satisfaction, and honesty. We must also speak to the perplexing feelings this engenders, and to the risk it poses to our relationships.

As I mentioned previously, sexual exclusivity is one way many couples define the distinctiveness of their bond. Take that away and for some the relationship is over. This is a controversial subject, and it's beyond the scope of this book to address the pros and cons of open relationships. What's important to remember is that you have to be comfortable with what you do, not what someone says you should do. Although timing and the reasons to open a relationship are important facts to consider, one arrangement can't be considered better than the other. What works for you and your lover is what's best. I will address the exceptions to this shortly.

Can discussing this lead to the dissolving your relationship? It's possible, if you and your partner have opposing, non-negotiable needs. Talking about it, however, may allow both of you to negotiate what was thought to be non-negotiable.

Not talking about it will also create trouble even if both of you are okay with outside sexual liaisons. Outside sex is not a simple event. Sex with whom, doing what, how often, when, where, under what circumstances? Much needs to be discussed.

When to Talk About This

Once you and the guy you're seeing have a commitment, this status should be made clear. Clarity avoids misunderstandings that lead to trouble. This is also a continuous process. Being monogamous this year doesn't mean you will want to remain that way next year. Monogamy versus open relationship is not a static issue but a dynamic that evolves as your relationship does.

When It's Not a Good Idea: Open Relationship in the Beginning

I said that one arrangement is not better than another, but when you consider an open relationship it does matter. At the outset of a developing relationship, it makes sense to be monogamous. This is the period when you are building trust and developing a sense of security. Sex with others at this juncture will interfere with that process. It will make it difficult to feel safe. Furthermore, intimacy, as wonderful as it is, is also unsettling. You have to cope with and transcend the fear of being less free and profoundly responsible to another human being. If the instant you sense this you seek sex with another to convince yourself that you're still "free," you will rob yourself of the opportunity to get through this developmental phase.

Once you have built a foundation and security with your partner, and significant time has passed, you may be able to consider an open relationship. If that's the way you feel, you should communicate that.

Open Relationship to Cure Problems

If you're having serious problems with your boyfriend, this is not the time to open your relationship. Doing so is analogous to a heterosexual couple having a baby to save their marriage. Not only is it a distraction that drives you away from dealing with your problems, it will make them worse. When a couple is in trouble, feelings of distrust and confusion surface, among many other painful emotions. An open relationship requires a high degree of trust and clarity about what you're doing and why. Involving others at this time is likely to aggravate your mutual distrust while confusing you further about your feelings toward your partner and where your relationship is headed.

Deciding on an Open Relationship

Let's say that you've been together with your boyfriend for three years. You have a satisfying, honest relationship. There's no doubt you love him and sex between the two of you has been good. But opportunities have arisen to be with other men. You never acted upon them because of your agreement. You were confident then as you are now that sex with them would have had no negative effect on your relationship. You are growing frustrated with this and are convinced that your agreement needs to be changed. How do you do this?

Be Sure Yourself

First make sure you really want this. An open relationship means *he will have sex with others also.* Of course you know that but have you though about it? Visualize it. He's out of town, for example, and you are about to go to sleep. You have not been able to reach him and you know that he may be in someone's bed right that moment. Is that okay? It may very well be, but just try to be sure by practicing the experience. What are your feelings? Jealousy, fear, anger, or who cares? Your visualization will not necessarily match the exact emotion, but it can give you a taste. Make sure you don't want to spit it out.

Easy Does It

So it is okay and you want to proceed. As much as you want this and have all the arguments why it can work, be aware that you're asking your partner to make a significant change. Present your case but don't expect an immediate positive response. Listen to what he says. That is the best way to understand what his concerns are and thus the best way to address them. Furthermore, if he balks, the worst thing you could do is resort to any kind of pejorative comments (you're up-tight, you just don't trust me; get over your Puritan values, etc.). If possible, ask him to commit to discuss the topic again later. He may simply need some time to process what you've told him.

Watch Out for Political Correctness; Create a Safe Atmosphere

There's pressure in our community to believe that an open relation-ship is simple, and to assume that something is wrong with the person who can't handle it. Your boyfriend, as well as yourself, may have bought into this. This is unhelpful because open relationships are not effortless, and a bad time to discover this is when you're living through one. Political correctness should have no standing in this conversation between you and your boyfriend. His feelings are legiti-mate, even if you don't agree with them. Only when you are both honest and tolerant of that honesty is there any chance that an open re-lationship can work.

Ethan, after being together with his lover Roger for two years, ap-proached Roger with this attitude. After telling Roger that he was in-terested in opening their relationship the following discussion ensued:

ETHAN: I want you to know that anything you feel about this is okay. And I am not demanding an open relationship. I just want to talk about it with you and see how you feel.

ROGER: Well, to be honest, I don't like the idea. Not at all.

ETHAN: Why?

ROGER: 'Cause I don't want any one else touching you.

ETHAN: Why not?

ROGER: Because I'm afraid I could lose you.

ETHAN: How would you lose me? It's about sex, not about emotion.

ROGER: Well, maybe you'll find him hotter than me and then you'll want to be with him. Why couldn't it lead to that? And how do you know it couldn't turn into emotion?

ETHAN: I love you. I don't want to love anyone else. This is about sex.

ROGER: Okay, you're right. I'm being stupid. Go ahead. It's okay.

ETHAN: Not so fast. You're not being stupid. This is a fear you have. It's not re-alistic because I know I'm not going to fall in love with anyone else. But you don't know that, so let's talk about it. I want you to feel reassured.

ROGER: I'm not sure you can do that.

ETHAN: Let's talk about it anyway.

ROGER: Well, I always thought that it was a miracle to have you. I've wondered why you would want to be with someone like me. I have feared that a day would come when I wouldn't be good enough. So I guess this is making me feel that way.

ETHAN: Wow! I didn't know you felt that way. Why wouldn't I want to be with someone like you? I think you're the best thing that ever happened to me.

ROGER: Really?

ETHAN: Yes, really, you silly boy.

ROGER: Now you're going to give me a swelled head [chuckling].

ETHAN: I want to do this because I want sex . . . I want to experience it with others. Sex. Not love. Not anything else.

ROGER: I know you're saying that but I still feel scared.

ETHAN: Hmm . . .

ROGER: What if we start doing it and I feel freaked out?

ETHAN: Then we talk about it again. And again if necessary. And it stops if it becomes unacceptable to you. If we're going to do this, I don't want you to be uncomfortable and I'll do whatever I need to convince you that this poses no threat to us. But you really have to be okay with it for it to be okay with me.

ROGER: That sounds pretty good, although I'm still not okay with it. I want to think about this. So no deal right now.

ETHAN: That sounds fair.

Real and Fake Threats

Outside sex, in itself, provides one of the lowest risks for falling in love with another. Sex for men (generally, not everyone) is easily divorced from emotional intimacy, so to believe that it will cause him or you to leave is fallacious. You are much more at risk when either of you go to work or walk the dog.

That being said, the absence of real risk doesn't discount psychological threat. Just because you won't fall in love with a trick doesn't mean your partner won't fear it. Worry such as this is only one of numerous emotions. Others may include the following:

- Jealousy
- Competitiveness
- Feeling left out
- Anger
- Ego deflation

The common denominator emotion from which all this derives is the *feeling of invasion into that the unique, primary, bond* that you have with your lover. He is *your* lover; you suck his dick, you kiss his mouth, you sleep next to him at night, you have an orgasm with him *and no one else does or should.* This is your territory and you don't want to share it with anyone. *These are possessive feelings.* Or course you don't possess him in the external world. Trying to really possess your lover is a prescription for relationship death. *That doesn't mean, however, that those feelings aren't there. We all have them, embarrassing and as politically incorrect as they may be. When you open a relationship, they are triggered. To successfully negotiate an open relationship means acknowledging that possessive feelings exist.* This enables both of you to deal with them, instead of hiding from them.

An imperative to managing these feelings is to create clear rules that establish clear boundaries. This works to preserve the sense of primacy between the two of you. There is no "one fits all" way to achieve this and couples create a wide variety of arrangements to meet their needs. For example, some couples will have one night a week when they can do what they want, no questions asked. Other couples decide that only when either of them is out of town can one have sex with others. Some couples insist that the sex must be anonymous. Others think it's okay to stay the night but never see him again. Some agree to talk about their experiences. Others agree to say nothing.

You have to do what feels right to you and your boyfriend. But keep this in mind: The less you let this activity resemble any kind of relationship, the less you integrate sexual partners into other aspects of you life, the better.

I recommend that you should never do the following.

- date or see a sexual partner on any kind of a regular basis
- exchange phone numbers
- have sex in your home, expecially a home you share with your boyfriend
- have sex with someone in your social circle
- have sex with someone at work
- have sex with an ex
- have any form of risky sex

Ongoing Discussion

An open relationship is not an agreement carved into stone. What you've consented to has to be experientially okay. Once you begin doing what you've decided to do, check in with each other. You may discover that what sounded good is not something you can actually live with. Don't hold your boyfriend to the agreement if he doesn't feel comfortable about it; simply re-negotiate.

What works this month may not work next year. Or you may be able in time to expand what you agreed upon. Some couples who would never dream of a threesome earlier in their relationship feel secure enough to experiment with it later on. An open relationship is a dynamic phenomenon that needs continuous attention and flexibility.

What if He Refuses to Have an Open Relationship?

If he will not, under any circumstances, accept an open relationship, what do you do? As I mentioned earlier, if each of you have opposite non-negotiable needs, your relationship will end or you will live in chronic misery. But before you come to this conclusion, it's imperative to make certain that your "need" to open the relationship is not a *desire*. This is not a word game. Not fulfilling a desire is something you could live with. You cannot live without fulfilling a need. Life is about choices, and although this may be a difficult one, you do have a choice. If you leave him, you can have sex with whomever you want, but he'll no longer be in your life. Is this what you want? What if sex with others is not all you thought it would be? You won't likely have the option of going back with him. This isn't to say that breaking up is always the wrong course of action. Just recognize that it's a major life decision, and that you should think long and hard before you take any action.

You should also consider that your boyfriend's refusal isn't necessarily forever. Feelings about monogamy often change as relationships develop and mature. Some couples go back and forth in their arrangements. Believing "I will never be able to have sex with another human being" is an overreaction that can panic you into a precipitous divorce.

Money

Money is up there with sex as one of the most complex issues to deal with in a relationship. Money has immense symbolic meaning, which creates numerous emotions. Money, in American society, is associated with power, freedom, happiness, and internal worth. Whether true or not, good or bad, this exists, and unless you have lived under a rock, these messages will affect you.

Some of us who are disgusted with how money affects our lives vow to do what we can to get away from its power. That's commendable, but if it leads you to believe that your relationship will be free of money's effects, you will be rudely awakened. Some of us find this difficult to acknowledge because admitting that we are affected by money makes us feel petty, cheap, shallow, etc. It's similar, in a way, to internalized homophobia. You may know on a conscious level that homophobic thoughts are illogical and bigoted and you may be embarrassed to admit that you still have them. However, a lifetime of being exposed to such messages makes that fact of life comprehensible. It's a force internally, as well as externally, to contend with. The same applies to money.

Different Attitudes Toward

Some folks feel very threatened by not having enough money and will watch every penny. Others don't have a lot of concern and will spend freely. This is not necessarily related to how much money one actually has.

It's easy to anticipate the conflict in a couple that has these divergent attitudes toward money, especially if the person who has more spends less, and vice versa. The terms tightwad and spendthrift are likely to be hurled at each other.

What's important to recognize is that the way we handle money is about the *relationship* we have with it. If you can understand this, you'll understand yourself and your partner and will not need to use pejorative terms that only create unnecessary conflict.

A person who is excessively concerned with money may be tormented that he will be without enough money even if it's implausible. Perhaps he grew up in poverty or with messages that continually conveyed to him the danger of being poor. It may also be his way of trying to feel in control or powerful. Sometimes rich, influential people feel deeply inadequate and having large sums of money is their way of trying to fend against those feelings.

Someone who has little money but spends it like water may be equally intimidated by money. He may be frustrated that he doesn't have enough and feel deprived, so he spends money he doesn't have as a way to ward off those feelings of deprivation. The point is that the way we handle money, even if it's extreme, is related to comprehensible emotions, not intrinsic personality flaws.

If you and your partner are stressing over money, you need to talk about it. We often treat money like a state secret and believe it is nobody's business but our own. Not when you're in a relationship! How each of you manages your individual funds also affects the relationship, and thus money becomes a relationship issue.

These are not the messages we are raised with. Some parents keep information about their individual funds a secret from both their spouses and children to their graves! Furthermore, having individual funds and the power to spend them in the manner you chose is a freedom issue. You may fear that talking about it will limit that freedom. It may to some degree, but if you're spending money on fancy clothes but can't come up with your share of the rent, this needs to be looked at.

Begin this conversation by getting away from name-calling and try to understand what each of you feels. It's also important to go inside and honestly address your own feelings.

When you bring this to the surface you will both better understand each other, which will cut down on the angst. It's also important to try to find a middle ground. Neither of you will undergo a personality reformation in relation to money, but you can each expand your comfort zones. If the way money is handled is causing the two of you problems, then some new arrangement has to be developed. It's in the best interests of both of you.

Joint Accounts

Putting money together is a major relationship step. Usually this happens only when significant time has passed and you are living together. It often makes sense on a pragmatic basis. If you have household expenses it becomes cumbersome to pay these from separate accounts.

In order to get to this level, you need to have resolved some of the previous issues I mentioned, if they exist. People with very diverging relationships with money who have found no meeting of the minds are unlikely to feel comfortable with pooling any funds.

Even if you have resolved those issues it's also important to sit down and clearly set up the parameters of a joint account agreement. First and foremost, do you actually trust your partner with access to your money? If you don't, acknowledge that now, embarrassing as that may be, because once he's involved with your money any lack of trust will become apparent whether you want it to be or not. This topic could eventually resolve if you and he are honest with your feelings.

Assuming you do trust him, exactly what will this money be spent on? Only the mortgage and food or will it also include entertainment? Will it include things that you do separately? Will both of you pay the bills and budget the money? Or will one of you take primary responsibility for this chore? Can the bill payer be depended upon to pay the bills on time?

Aside from pragmatic considerations, successful pooling of funds is relationship enhancing. It's a tangible declaration that you are, indeed, a couple.

That being said, it's still important to have your own money. The healthiest of relationships are a balance between "merging" and individuation. Having your own money to buy what you want (within the limits of your relationship responsibilities indicated previously) helps maintain that balance.

Major Difference in Income

Some men in a relationship have vastly different incomes. The question then arises as how to handle this. If you make $30,000 a year and your lover earns $150,000 you obviously don't have equal buying power. If he wants to go to expensive restaurants and on pricey vacations and live in a fancy home, you simply can't contribute equally.

Income differences need to be frankly discussed. If he says he's okay with paying most expenses, is that the end of the discussion? I would say no. Such diverging incomes present challenges whether we like it or not. As free as he may be with his money, he may come to resent paying for everything. This may rear its ugly head at a time when your relationship is having challenges, making it a very ugly head indeed.

If you are the recipient of his generosity you may consider yourself fortunate until you feel that you owe him and are not really free. Whether we like it or not and as irrational as it can be, money is related to power, control, and lots of confusing intense emotions. He may mean well and really feel comfortable with paying for everything when he tells you this, but in the long run it simply will not work.

A number of issues can be negotiated. Perhaps he needs to scale down some of his high life to accommodate you. If he doesn't want to do that then you must find creative ways to strike a balance. Perhaps on occasion you pay for dinner or take him on a vacation. You can't do it as often or as elaboratly as he can, but you still can do it. If he's paying for an expensive home, than perhaps you can have the role of doing the work of decorating it or maintaining it. This all must be discussed and you need to come to an agreement. It's imperative that you don't feel you're doing subservient work to earn your keep but that you are making an important contribution that *you want to make*. Furthermore, it should be addressed as often as necessary that his decision to pay for more is a voluntary decision and that you don't "owe him." You must believe that as much as he needs to.

Make no mistake about this: extremely disparate incomes are a significant challenge that may not be overcome. If you don't recognize the challenge and work on a resolution, it will surely overwhelm both of you.

Insecurity About Being Loved

Being in love is *the* defining characteristic of relationships we call romantic. We can love our parents, love our friends, and even love the human race. But being in love in that special way is reserved, well, for your lover!

Defining it is difficult because it's an emotional state that in some ways transcends the limits of language. Yet it's a condition we clearly recognize when present and also when missing.

The people in relationships have to stay in love in order for the relationship to remain viable. Years of strife between two people sometimes erodes the feeling to the point of no return. Sometimes there is no strife but the normal course of human change results in love dissolving nonetheless.

Talking about this can be one of the scariest things a couple can do. To learn your partner is no longer in love with you is not only a statement that your relationship is over, it's also a terrible assault on your ego. Equally agonizing is telling someone you've loved that you no longer love him. Yet if this is happening it needs to be addressed because a loveless relationship that spans years and even decades is a waste of two lives. You'll both end up bitter and perhaps hating each other.

Another side to this issue is that you may fear that your partner has fallen out of love with you when he has not. If this doesn't get addressed, a nonissue can morph into a serious problem.

Couples can go through hard times when it may seem that love has disapated, but being buried under the onslaught of life's problems is very different from love no longer existing.

Jake and Harry, a couple in their late forties who live in Ann Arbor, Michigan, had a year and a half of unremitting bad fortune. They had been together at that point for more than ten years.

Within three months Jake's father, his best friend, and a co-worker died. His dad was ill with Alzheimer's disease for a number of years so his death did not come as a shock, but it cut a big hole in his life. Then came the domino nightmare. A week later his friend was killed in a motorcycle accident and three days later his co-worker died of a heart attack at work right in front of him. Before Harry had a moment to a take a breath and try to be there for Jake, he, Harry, lost his job due to downsizing and outsourcing at his company. Then, as if there was a cosmic vendetta out to screw both of them, Harry became a victim of identity fraud. Driving home from the police station and the bank a day after he learned that he had "bought two trucks," he totaled his car. On television this scenario would have been a bad comic soap opera, but it was actually happening to them and it certainly was no laughing matter.

Viewing this from the outside, it's obvious that the pressures on them were enormous, and they spilled over to their relationship. But living in the middle of it made nothing obvious to them. Each man needed the other to be there for him and neither could; each resented this situation. They began blaming each other for being emotionally unavailable and "not giving a shit." They argued over whose plight was worse as they grew more bitter and resentful with each other. Sex went out the window along with any semblance of civility.

When they finally consulted a therapist, both were convinced that the other no longer loved him and that their relationship was over. They expected the therapist to help them disengage. When they were able to pull back and get some emotional space from their situation, they were able to see that the events were the issues, not each other. They were very much in love but had felt so out of control that the only "control" they were able to achieve was to blame the other for their woes. In therapy they were able to reaffirm their love for each other. This was the beginning of the healing process as they began to accept that they had no control over what had happened to both of them. They were ready to move on.

Your problems don't have to be as dramatic as Jake and Harry's to cause stress to distance you from your lover. Twenty-first-century life is, unfortunately, the definition of stress. From unbounded job obligations that erode the quantity and quality of free time, to pagers and cell phones that keep us on electronic leashes, to the ever-increasing pace and pressure to get ahead, do more with less, in less time, we are drowning in stress. Pulling away from the one you love is a comprehensible reaction because so much aggravation drains your emotional energy.

The task is to recognize this and not confuse it with falling out of love. You need to talk about what is happening and to resist the temptation to take out your frustrations on your lover. You may also have to find a way to give your middle finger to the twenty-first century. Maybe all that getting ahead is not worth it. Maybe "getting ahead" is just getting you ahead of others to the cemetery. Perhaps you need to set boundaries at your job, and if that doesn't work, to leave your job. As I said earlier, life is about choices. Think about this: Do you want to make choices that cause your relationship to burn out when the love is still flourishing?

Addiction

> . . . I wasn't too sure if I was talking to him or the drug.
>
> Diego, 28, customer service representative
> Tucson, Arizona

Addiction, whether it is to a substance or something else, will destroy your relationship and possibly your life. An addiction is a form of out of control behavior that delivers quick-fix gratification at the cost of massive, long-term destruction. What's unique about addiction is that it *cannot, ever, under any circumstances,* co-exist with healthy functioning. Addictions *replace* life. They are much like alien forces that invade bodies in those horror flicks. The person looks the same but it's no longer him. In time, addictions even replace the physical appearance. And it isn't pretty when that happens.

In drug addiction, life revolves around getting the substance. Friends, lovers, finances, jobs, obligations, health, and dignity all crash and burn as the almighty drug reigns supreme. Lying, cheating, stealing, and manipulating the ones you used to be able to love become second nature. Getting high is all that matters.

Addiction does not involve just alcohol and other drugs. You can be addicted to sex, food, work, gambling, and the list doesn't stop there.

It's beyond the scope of this book to comprehensively examine the subject matter of addiction. But this much is certain: if you're an addict and you don't get competent, professional help, you're going down. If you're the lover of an addict who refuses help, you need to leave him or you're going to go down with him.

One of the hallmarks of addiction is denial. Although this is an overused term, it's appropriate in this context. Simply put, denial means one is unable to acknowledge and take any responsibility for the obsessive and highly destructive nature of one's behavior. It's living in a world of emotional make believe in which repeated blackouts and DUIs are called "social drinking." Losing your job, lover, friends, and home is not because of crack, it's because you live in LA. Moving will change everything. Compulsive sex in public toilets and getting arrested is "just sex and the homophobic police." Losing $100,000 in Vegas is just a "bad streak."

Addictions, particularly to chemicals and sex, are formidable challenges in the LGBT community. Not only are they widespread, but the social context in which we live adds to the problem. Sex, drugs, and rock and roll are part of our LGBT culture, and they aren't going anywhere. In such an environment it becomes difficult to discern the blurry line between recreation and addiction. Add denial and it's easy to see why this topic doesn't get adequately addressed.

If you have any questions about your behavior, or if others are expressing concern, you should check in with an expert. It doesn't mean that you're an addict, but it won't hurt to clarify the situation.

Indications of potential serious problems include the following:

- Having unsafe sex while drinking or using other drugs
- Missing work because of the behavior (e.g., being too hung over to go to work, being out all night in sex clubs, or meeting sex partners online)
- Feeling increasingly irritable or having outbursts that are out of character
- Getting ill, unexplained loss of weight, feeling run down
- Erratic sleep patterns
- Needing immediate anonymous sex when feeling frightened or depressed or angry or bored
- Making a decision to refrain from the behavior only to discover that you "have to" go back to it
- Feeling guilty after engaging in the behavior
- Cheating on your boyfriend repeatedly and not wanting to
- Getting turned on by sex in public places that puts you at risk for being arrested
- Being arrested for public sex
- Long-time friends disappearing from your life, and friendships that revolve around partying becoming prominent in your life
- Binges
- Getting behind in your financial obligations because large sums of money are needed to fund your behavior
- A general feeling that your life is out of control

This list is by no means exhaustive. Any troubling behavior that seems to involve pleasure along with destruction with a feeling of compulsivity requires further exploration.

If you are the partner of someone who has an addiction problem you are in a terribly painful place. To love someone who is no longer himself and is self-destructing is terrifying and paralyzing. You also probably know that you are no match for his addiction, yet there could be a "conspiracy of silence" in your home. The reasons may include:

- You are also addicted and both of you are in mutual denial.
- You don't want to acknowledge that someone you love is so terribly out of control and in a downward spiral.
- You don't want to accept that your relationship may have to end.
- You feel intimidated because he has told you to shut up and get off his back when you've confronted him in the past.
- He becomes violent or runs out of the house if you bring up the topic.
- He denies with gasping sincerity that he's not doing what you think he's doing.
- You buy into his excuses for stress causing him to drink or your lack of giving good sex as a reason why he has to have so much sex with others.
- You feel like a prude because you're not into the scene (doing drugs, for example) and feel that his friends and even your own will criticize you for overreacting and being "un-cool."
- You feel very confused about your feelings.
- You really are not sure if he has a problem. Maybe you think that you have the problem.

Bear in mind that you don't need to be right and no one is expecting you to be an addiction counselor. If something about what he is doing makes you feel uncomfortable, that, in itself, legitimizes the need to address it. Perhaps it's not an addiction; he discuses it with you, he modifies his behavior, you're no longer worried, and the problem is resolved. Fine. However, if he refuses to discuss it or does talk but nothing changes then a professional is needed. Although some relationship problems do not require therapy, this is *not* one of them. Because addictive behavior is so complex and confusing and denial is so much part of the picture, a competent, impartial, professional trained in addiction problems *with gay men* is necessary. If he refuses to see a professional, you should go alone. You can receive information and learn what to do to save yourself if he won't save himself.

Relationship Ambivalence

Being in a serious relationship presents challenges we don't endure when single. A relationship restricts freedom. Even in the most well-balanced unions, major life decisions are made as a couple. Your dream may be to live in Paris, but you can't actualize that dream unless your partner will live there also. Relationships also require never-ending compromise. They make us vulnerable, confused on occasion, and emotionally exposed. As we age we change, and need to work at accommodating those transitions.

This is not easy and it's foolhardy to think that ambivalence doesn't creep into the picture. Sometimes you may wish that you didn't ever have to see his face again and can simply drink a beer and fart in peace.

> ... you can't be with someone for seven years and not have some point at which they're bored with you and you're bored with them. That's probably one of the most difficult things you can actually say out loud to someone.
>
> Christian, 36, real estate agent
> Miami Beach, Florida

This, of course, doesn't mean you want to break up, or don't value the love you have. But experiencing ambivalence or believing your partner is unsure can be scary. In light of the widespread belief among gay men that gay relationships don't last, this becomes a taboo subject.

Ambivalence is common, and keeping the subject unmentionable makes it more powerful than it is. Once you can appreciate that it's a foreseeable part of a relationship, particularly in long-term relationships, it's not so threatening.

Discussing your ambivalence may lead to positive changes. Long-term love can lead to long-term boredom. We can get comfortable to the point of making life stale. Marriage is not a static, guaranteed state but a dynamic process that needs continuous support. We often forget this or stop caring in our comfort. You car will not survive without maintenance and neither will your relationship. Ambivalence can grow from the predictability of life and taking one's partner for granted. By talking frankly about this, change can happen. There's no law in the universe decreeing that you can't look special for your boyfriend, or must have the same kind of sex, or can't surprise him with flowers, or dinner, or putting on his coat. Addressing these problems could enhance the quality of your relationship.

Ambivalence can also come about from acute feeling states. This is very different from what I have just described. An "acute feeling

state" as I am defining it here is an intense emotion related to a negative environmental stressor. For example, you have a bad fight with
your boyfriend. You feel no love for him *at that moment* and question
why you are with him. Or you "decide" to break up. Moment is the
operative word. Your feeling, while very intense, is likely to pass
once the anger does. The feeling, however, can confuse you because
at that moment reality and feeling appear to be the same. This is the
time *not* to share this with your partner, and certainly not to act upon
it. Some couples do that with devastating consequences. Recognizing
that the feeling is not an accurate depiction of reality should help you
accept it for what it is; something that has no significance and will
pass.

Feelings, and Men and Feelings

This is a good segue to the topic of feelings and *men and feelings*.
Relationships, on the whole, are about feelings. Feelings of love, happiness, vulnerability, anger, pleasure, fear, and six to twenty million
others. Relationships are born from, operate from, and thrive on feelings. As men, we have a serious problem. Male socialization in our
culture teaches us to discard, avoid, repress, deny and not even know
our feelings. Feelings are for sissies. "Real" men, the "red-blooded
American kind," walk tall, take charge, fear nothing, and don't waste
time with "female stuff." Obviously, this is a wild generalization, but
it's born from real problems we men experience. So how are we able
to have loving relationships? The next chapter addresses this.

Chapter 5

How to Stop Running
from Your Male Feelings

Feelings are the essence of life. Human beings have feelings, and they formulate, color, and deepen the journey of existence. The view of a golden sunset, the bond with a friend, or the experience of creativity would be meaningless without human feelings. Love would cease to exist.

Delegitimizing Feelings

We belittle feelings in our culture and sometimes deny that they exist. Feelings are "soft" and "for sissies." What matters is *what is done, what can be measured, what is produced.* We perceive wealthy people as having it all, for example, without giving much thought about their experience of feelings.

Simon and Garfunkel's "Richard Cory" comes to mind. Richard Cory is a prosperous, influential man and the singer laments because he's poor and works in Richard Cory's factory. He tells us that Richard Cory has "everything," until the last lines of the song remind us of the power of feelings:

So my mind was filled with wonder when the evening headlines read:

Richard Cory went home last night and put a bullet through his head.[1]

---

[1]From the song "Richard Cory," written by Paul Simon and produced by Bob Johnson. Original release 1966 on the album *Sounds of Silence,* perfomed by Simon and Garfunkel. Columbia Records. *Source:* "The Essential Simon and Garfunkel" (album on the Web).

Feelings are also absurdly ignored. A comical example of this is when a judge orders a statement in front of a jury to be "stricken." The jury is ordered to disregard what has been said, but does anyone really believe that the feelings engendered by a powerful statement can just be "stricken?" Will that have no effect on the jury's ultimate decision?

Men and Feelings

> . . . males in this society get the message that it's better not to be vulnerable to other people, especially other males. They're socialized to be competitive as opposed to being vulnerable and collaborative. Values like that (which) males grow up with make it difficult when there's a couple comprised of two males.
>
> Betty Berzon, PhD, private practice
> Los Angeles, California

Although we have difficulty dealing with feelings as a society, this is particularly problematic for men. Males are socialized from a very early age into avoiding, disregarding, repressing, and literally losing their ability to identify and understand feelings. Little boys are told to "be a man" to "grow up" to "stop being a sissy" when showing emotion, particularly fear or sadness.

> . . . that's the way my father, my family, defined what it meant to be male. . . . The way they defined being male was to be tough, to be strong, to not express your feelings. . . . My grandmother passed away when I was thirteen. She just dropped dead . . . my father didn't cry . . . three years later he cried. We had to take him to the emergency room because he had such an emotional reaction at that point . . .
>
> Christian, 36, real estate agent
> Miami Beach, Florida

> . . . my grandmother, she always said, don't let people know that you're scared, that you're hurt, just hide it as much as you can . . . don't let anybody know that you're weak . . .
>
> Diego, 28, customer service representative
> Tucson, Arizona

These toxic ideas come from everywhere: parents, siblings, relatives, teachers, peers, the media, sports heroes, etc. Boys/men are also bombarded with messages that they should be:

- Powerful
- Tough
- Strong
- Resilient
- Fearless
- In control
- In charge
- Dominant
- Competitive
- Fighters
- Protectors
- Providers
- Violent
- Masculine
- Muscular
- Threatening
- Logical
- Levelheaded
- Big
- Winners
- Devoid of fear, regret, sadness, and tears

We pay dearly for this emotional poisoning.

If you distort your humanity into this caricature, you encase your feelings in a vault. If your feelings are buried you miss out on life. Even painful feelings enrich us. Crying, for example, is emotionally cathartic; it's superior to being "frozen." Furthermore, being shut down doesn't really protect you from pain. In fact, the suffering is worse. You carry a global sense of discomfort without understanding what is going on. This is actually a state of being out of control, which ironically, is the last thing many men want.

Not only are such men uncomfortable but their misery has no company. No one wants to comfort a snarling, stone-faced person who says "leave me alone—I'm fine." Lack of support then serves to deepen their pain.

Never Wrong

One grim derivative of this mind-set is that it prevents men from acknowledging that they made a mistake. To do so would be admitting that they're not perfect, not always in control. It would mean reflecting on one's behavior and feelings and experiencing remorse. This is the antithesis to the edicts of male socialization.

> . . . with gay male couples the issue of control is often a very important one; it's often kind of ground zero for the problems in the relationship. I find that much more with male couples than with lesbian couples.
>
> Betty Berzon, PhD, private practice
> Los Angeles, California

> I have to be the strong one in our relationship . . . if the person who's supposed to be in charge can't hold it together, then what does that mean for the rest of us?
>
> Christian, 36, real estate agent
> Miami Beach, Florida

This is not good for relationships—not good at all.

Ironically, and I could say even tragically, the ability to admit mistakes is a requisite for a relationship to work. We are all mistaken at times (many times!) and to never be able to admit that creates a non-reality in the life of the relationship that can prevail for just so long. When you put two men together you can have a chronic war of blame, and continual vying for dominance that sucks the joy and literal life out of their relationship. The relationship becomes an Olympic competition, not the safe haven for two men who love each other. The result is disaster. This is why it's so important for men to "get over their male feelings." More to the point, they have to learn how to deal with feelings. The good news is that it can be accomplished.

The Myth of Wishing Away Feelings

Feelings that don't get accessed, acknowledged, and dealt with do not go away. Like hungry dogs locked in the basement, they grow stronger in their determination to get out. The danger with this is that *they will ultimately come out, likely in behavior that is destructive.* Unaddressed anger can manifest in explosive violence. Fear of vulnerability can result in the end of a relationship that did not have to end. One of the biggest fallacies of male socialization is the belief that you can simply wish a feeling out of existence. On the contrary, it will not only remain, it will end up controlling you.

Gay Men and Feelings

Homophobia and aspects of our lifestyle serve to further complicate our issues with feelings. We, like our heterosexual brothers, are also the victims of male socialization, but we have additional problems. Despite the enlightenment of the past twenty-five years or so our membership in the "real men's club" is still questionable. Some of us don't care, but for others membership is vital. For these folks the tenets of toxic male socialization are exceedingly important because it's what they feel they must live by in order to be acceptable. Such gay men may be more caught up in the need to divorce themselves from their feelings than the archetypal straight, macho, homophobic male.

> ...knowing that [you're gay] and living in a culture that does not accept that, you're constantly . . . trying to be something that you're not. . . . Men, for the most part, are taught . . . suppress your feelings; don't show emotion; that's not very strong; that's very weak. . . . You being a male—and then being a gay male on top of it—there's just that conflict that comes into the relationship . . . you have that wall there . . .
>
> Javon, 35, writer
> New Orleans, Louisiana

Consider these additional challenges. Growing up immersed in homophobia, we learned, early in life, that our erotic feelings needed to be hidden. We thus learned to compartmentalize. We could be gay in the protection of our community but out there in the rest of the world we had to play straight. Much of course is different and rapidly transforming today, but the changes we enjoy in this early part of the twenty-first-century are far too new and incomplete to declare that this legacy is gone. It's still here; we still hide and compartmentalize. The process is, unfortunately, second nature to many of us. Concealing and repressing one set of powerful emotions makes doing the same to other feelings equally effortless and even automatic.

The custom of no strings attached, nonemotionally involved sex, a significant feature of gay male culture, presents still another dilemma. This practice certainly provides a playground of sexual encounters that is terribly exciting and pleasurable, but it can also negatively affect how you deal with feelings. If you have been having one-night stands, and sex-club sex for years, and have done nothing else, you have been relating to gay men devoid of complex feelings, or perhaps of any feelings. You have been having the experience of physical intimacy with no emotional intimacy. This is another form of compartmentalization. It creates further detachment from being able to access and understand your feelings.

Gay Couples

Given all this baggage (I would say a few steamer trunks!), how then do we create viable relationships?

You must begin by buying into the fact that feelings are extremely important in relationships. You need to recognize that dealing with feelings is a challenge that can be overcome. As you understand how emotions operate and are willing to "risk" opening up, your communication will improve as will your relationship.

What Are Feelings?

What we label as a feeling may actually be something else. For example, let's say you come home from work, you say hello to your boyfriend, and he ignores you. He's working on the computer and barely acknowledges you're there. What are you feeling? To say "I feel he's slighting me" is not expressing a feeling—it's a expressing your critique of his behavior. *Feelings are about oneself; what is going on inside oneself, which* may or may not be related to the external world. For example, you can feel sad with no "sad" external event because you're depressed. In the previous example, you may feel frustrated, dejected, unimportant, unloved *in relation* to his behavior but *you are not feeling what he is, or is not, doing.* This distinction is vital in couple communication. When you express feelings, you identify the heart of what is going on inside you, what is bothering you, and it's something that your partner is likely to relate to. If you express a critique of his behavior, you are obscuring your feelings and simulta-neously expressing what is likely to be viewed by him as criticism. This then produces defensiveness, which derails communication.

Ownership of Feelings

A similar problem arises when ownership of feelings is confused.

One of the most misunderstood ideas is that someone, other than yourself, *creates* your feelings. It's not uncommon for people to say "he *makes* me angry, sad, upset, fearful, etc." That notion implies that someone outside of oneself is in control of one's emotions. The belief is erroneous because we all react in different ways to external stimuli. Those reactions, one class of which are feelings, are *created by the in-dividual experiencing the feelings* based on who that person is. Who that person "is" means the complex of experience and biology that makes each one of us unique. Someone speaking loudly, for example, may frighten you, irritate someone else, yet amuse another person. The external variable, loud talking, is the same for the three of you, but each of you have different feelings relative to the stimulus.

This doesn't mean that feelings spring from nothingness. In the hy-pothetical example of you not being greeted by your boyfriend after you come home from work, it's reasonable conjecture that you will feel hurt. Your feelings are related to his behavior. *But related, nei-ther controlled by nor owned by him.* Why is this distinction so im-portant? Because it's the fact of the matter, and when you deal in real-ity you are empowered. Ownership of feelings means that you have a choice. You can choose your reaction, including choosing not to have a boyfriend who doesn't greet you. You have the power; you are not at his mercy. Furthermore, when you take responsibility for your feel-ings, you avoid the blame game, which is the surest way to decimate communication. In this example, your boyfriend may be lost in thought, not feel well, be worried about something, etc., *but have no intention or even awareness that you are feeling hurt.* If he is slammed with "you are hurting me; you're pissing me off; you're making me feel like shit," he may not have the foggiest idea of what you are talking about and automatically go into defensive posture. "Hurting you?" he may thunder. "Can't you see I'm busy? You have no respect for me!" could be his response. On the other hand, if you say, "I feel hurt when I come home from work and you don't say hello," the blame is turned off, negotiation is requested, and the possibility of resolution is exceedingly more likely.

Nonjudgment

Feelings are visceral human experiences that have nothing to do with right or wrong, good or bad, moral or immoral. Feelings can be traced to external events such as in the previous example, yet other times they are mystifying. Moreover, they don't necessarily have anything to do with logic. Feelings can come and go, be in conflict yet exist simultaneously, disappear for no apparent reason and then reappear again. They live in a world of their own.

In our judgment-obsessed society, this is hard for many to embrace. We often believe that we have to justify our feelings and feel guilty for having "wrong" or "bad" or "nasty" feelings. Feelings are also very distinct from actions. Although any rational-thinking person knows this, on an emotional level this is also challenging to accept. For example, we may feel rage toward someone, imagine the person being run over by a tractor-trailer, and then feel we have done something terrible.

> . . . I was afraid of my emotions and my feelings. I felt that they were wrong or that they would hurt him.
>
> Aidan, 37, physical therapist
> Tampa, Florida

To access feelings you must first suspend judgment. If a feeling is too terrible to have, you are likely to suppress it. Letting go of judgment is easier said then done. However, if you can repeatedly remind yourself that feelings themselves *do nothing,* that they are there whether you like them or not, you may be able to give yourself permission to feel without shame.

Fear of Feelings

Some folks fear that their feelings can turn into actions and therefore suppress them in an effort to prevent that. You may fight feelings of sexual attraction or feelings of violence. Paradoxically, the more you are in touch with your feelings, the less likely they will result in inappropriate actions. Understanding your feelings gives you distance and clarity about what is making you tick. That facilitates control over what you want to do in relation to what you feel. When you can take the "risk" to experience feelings and then observe how this empowers you, your fear of knowing your feelings is likely to decrease.

Sense of No Control

Feelings do not exist in the objective, material world. You cannot hold a feeling in your hand or view it with your eyes. They are hypothetical constructs. We experience them as internal sensations that are illogical, shifting, fleeting, and confusing. This means that acknowledging one's feelings can feel out of control. This is why men so often instinctively subjugate feelings. Men "need" to be in control, which means they require lead encasings around their feelings. The way out of this abyss is to let go of the control.

This brings us to an interesting question. Why do men feel such a strong need to control? We know it develops from male socialization, but what's the reason, the payoff? What's so terrible if you aren't in control? Male socialization imparts the edict that lack of control means vulnerability, which therefore means extreme danger. Why? Men are fighters, protectors, providers, winners, problem solvers, doers. The identity of a man is derived from his ability to control. Without being in control, he cannot be a fighter, winner, provider, doer, etc. He loses his identity, along with his sense of homeostasis and safety. In this mind-set, being out of control is about as good as being dead.

This kind of thinking rises terribly close to the level of delusion. In point of fact *the entire human race is in far, far less control than we think. The massive changes in technology and humankind's increased ability to manipulate the environment have given us a faulty sense of power.* Most control is an illusion. When you're hit with a smack of reality (you are diagnosed with terminal cancer at thirty-two; your child drowns; you're fired after working twenty years at the same company) you experience the rude awakening of just how little control you really have.

If you can begin to appreciate this fact, as disturbing as it may seem at first, you will be more inclined to let go because you'll realize you're essentially letting go of an *illusion*. You have been sold a false bill of goods; you have been lied to. You really have no control over your boyfriend loving you, your relationship lasting, your health remaining good, or even if you will come home alive from work tonight. You do what you can to minimize the chances of a disaster but in the final analysis *you really are not in control.*

And despite your lack of control you're still here. You're alive; you eat, breathe, love, and fuck, which means that not being in control doesn't signify imminent disaster. *You can be not in control and still be fine. You don't need that control.* Taking this stance will create wonders for your ability to deal with your feelings, your relationship, and your life.

Practicing Being Out of Control

If you can practice letting go of trying to control events in the physical world, it will make it easier for you to accept feelings, which by definition will be experienced as out of your control. Numerous opportunities abound in everyday life to let go of what you're not controlling anyway. Being stuck in traffic is a perfect opportunity. The next time it happens, do the following (you can substitute being stuck in the subway or on a bus, for those of you who live in NYC):

Take a few slow, deep breaths and begin to observe the internal chatter streaking through your mind. Try as much as you can to distance yourself from your thoughts. I am assuming you are not moving at all or very slowly. *(Do not do this if in any way this will distract you from concentrating on the road.)* The thoughts are probably moving rapidly through your mind: *This is horrible; this is stupid; why are all these stupid cars here? Why isn't traffic moving? When is it going to move? Maybe it'll never move. This is killing my schedule. This is killing me. Why the hell do I live in this idiotic city? I'll kill the next guy that tries to get in front of me.*

Begin to replace those thoughts (as you are physiologically calming down from the breathing) with: *Let go; you have no control over this. Let it go, you cannot control this. You have no responsibility in this; it will move when it's ready to move. Let it go; let it go; let it go.* Repeat those phases as many times as you need to. Continue to breath deeply and slowly.

Another opportunity is when your boyfriend wants to do something that you don't want him to do. The kind of situation I'm referring to will not impact you directly (like a vacation you would go on together) but something that he wants to do by himself for himself. Let's say he decides to buy a suit for $600. You're aware that he doesn't have much money. You know he doesn't need the suit, and probably will never wear it, but he wants it and he told you he's buying it. As intuitive as it will feel for you to scream out "Are you out of your mind?" and as much as you want to save him from himself, just say nothing. Repeat: *let go and say nothing. Let him do what he wants to do.* Tell yourself that it's his decision, that you rightly don't have any control over his decisions, and that his decisions are not your responsibility.

It will probably be difficult when you first try this. But if you repeatedly let go of situations that you can't control anyway, you will discover that it feels good to let go, that it's a relief when you "submit" to forces that you have no control over. You'll also realize that nothing terrible has happened. The traffic eventually does move; your boyfriend still has money to eat. And you'll discover that you can start getting to know your feelings, which will help you communicate with the man you love.

Accessing, Understanding, and Dealing with Your Feelings

Your difficulty with feelings is likely to manifest when you have a powerful reaction to something and are confused as to why you're feeling this way. This becomes a perfect opportunity to put into practice the issues previously discussed (nonjudgment of feelings, letting go of fear that they will cause you to act out, embrace "being out of control," etc.) and get in touch with what's going on. Let's look at what happened between Simon and Victor.

Simon and Victor are a couple living in Spokane, Washington, and have been together for eight years. They are professional men both in their mid-thirties. One Tuesday morning in the early Spring before they were both leaving for work, Victor told Simon that he would be getting home late that evening because he was going to a movie with his friend Marvin. Simon and Victor often made last-minute announcements like this and neither had a problem with it. Not when it came to Victor getting together with Marvin, however.

SIMON: I'd rather you don't go . . . tonight.

VICTOR: What?

SIMON: I want you home tonight. I want to have dinner with you. We seem to not have had any time together lately.

VICTOR: You know this happens whenever I want to spend some time with Marvin.

SIMON: No, I mean this . . . I have not seen much of you lately.

VICTOR: That's not the issue, Simon.

SIMON: Okay. I can't stand that bastard. But I really would like to be with you tonight. You can set it up with him for another time.

VICTOR: [walking out the front door]: I'll be home at about eleven. There's plenty of food in the refrigerator.

Simon felt frustrated and fantasized about hitting Marvin. He imagined coming home that evening to an empty house and felt a sour sensation in his gut. He had no fear that they were having sex—they had been platonic friends since college and Marvin was not Victor's type, yet it was bugging him. He hated Marvin's chatty persona and high-pitched voice, but he knew there was more to it than that. But what was it? It was true that he *never* liked it when Victor got together with him and he always tried to stop it. He never wanted to join them either. *What is going on?* he thought, as he locked their front door and proceeded to drive to work.

That evening Simon did not come home directly from work but instead met a friend for dinner and played a few games of pool. He knew he was doing this to get his mind off the fact that Victor was with Marvin and it worked. He arrived home about half an hour after Victor. His anger was gone and Victor, not wanting to set him off, didn't mention his evening with Marvin. They both went to sleep without any incident.

The next morning Simon couldn't get this off his mind. Victor was as pleasant as ever and said nothing about the incident. It was if he had become used to it. But Simon had not. He didn't want to go through this again. He recognized that Marvin was Victor's friend and he was going to have to find a way to live with this, but he'd first have to figure out what was really bothering him. He made a choice to risk all his comfort with staying away from his feelings and try to get in touch with them.

The following evening Victor had to work late so Simon planned to spend some time by himself at home. He turned off the TV, unplugged all of the phones, and turned off his cell phone and pager. He dimmed the light in his study and put on some soothing, low-volume music. He put himself into a relaxed state (after taking a bath and doing some breathing exercises) and sat in his favorite leather chair. He dressed in loose cotton sweat pants and a soft flannel pullover and soft cotton socks. He was very comfortable.

He had a faint awareness that his dislike for Marvin, besides his voice and bubbly personality, had something to do with his longtime friendship with Victor. So this is where he began. *"What did that long history between them mean to him?"* he asked himself. He began to focus his attention toward himself, toward his body. *"What do I feel in my bones about this?"* he asked himself. He made a conscious effort to let go of any judgment of his feelings and any need to justify or make them rational and simply asked himself what he *felt* when he thought of Marvin and Victor being together. Almost immediately he got in touch with powerful feelings of rage shortly followed by feelings of jealousy followed by a painful feeling of being left out and abandoned. He then began connecting this to his feelings he had as a child, feelings he never fully acknowledged. His family relocated often (his dad had problems keeping a job and moved the family around the country repeatedly) and Simon had trouble making friends. He always seemed to be the new kid on the block and lacked the history of friendship the other kids had among themselves. He sensed he was the "odd ball" and "the extra one." He felt "less than" and "left out." He was terribly jealous of the other boys and his self-esteem was close to nonexistent. He then realized that this was the precise set of feelings he was experiencing with Marvin. It mattered not that he, Simon, was Victor's lover. *On a feeling level he was "left out" of that special friendship they had since college. He was alone again and felt empty and insignificant.* His realization was upsetting as it was liberating. This didn't offer an instant solution but it was a beginning—it would enable him to commence a rational dialogue with Victor about what was really going on. He did. This grew their intimacy, as Victor now understood what was underneath his complaints about Marvin. Both recognized that Victor's friendship with Marvin would have to continue. They acknowledged that any change in his relationship with Marvin would be very unhealthy for them as a couple. Victor was particularly sensitive about the issue, however, and Simon appreciated this. It was kind of a quiet respect for Simon's difficulty whenever he got together with Marvin. Simon entered therapy to deal with this and a number of other issues. Their relationship flourished.

You and Your Lover

Let's assume you're experiencing some confusion with your feelings in relation to your boyfriend? What can you do?

As in the example with Simon, you need to let go of judgment and "rationality" and control, and point your senses inside. This should be done when you're alone and feeling calm and comfortable. Going inside, of course, starts with reviewing what happened, the external "facts" of the situation. However, as soon as you begin judging and focusing on your lover you're beginning to waste your time. Perhaps he yelled at you in a restaurant and walked out on you. Certainly you can make a case for why that's inappropriate. But that's not what this process is about. Your endeavor is to determine how you felt when this happened.

As you examine feelings, you will discover that many feelings are layered. Simply put, one feeling is predicated on another, deeper one. For example, you may feel angry, because you feel hurt, because you feel embarrassed, because you feel terrified. As you reflect and identify a feeling, say to yourself *"I feel this because . . ."* to ascertain if other feelings are underneath. *Don't get crazy with this process*—theoretically you can go on forever. You simply want to determine if some deeper feelings are present.

Be careful to label feelings properly. "He cheated me" is not a feeling; "I felt cheated" is. Someone else's action is not a feeling. That is why it's so important to use "I" when describing your feeling. If you improperly label feelings, you will be getting away from your emotional experience.

The following is a list of some feelings that may come up when there's stress between you and your partner. It's a small sample of what you can experience, but it may help jump-start this process. Those feelings include:

- Fear
- Jealousy
- Anger
- Loss
- Vulnerability

- Closed off
- Numbness
- Guilt
- Powerlessness
- Emptiness
- Insignificant
- Weak
- Foolish
- Small
- Helpless
- Trapped
- Out of control
- Unable
- Dependent
- Sad
- Frightened
- Dirty

Anger and Relationships

Anger exists is all relationships. It's part of being human. Nonetheless, it's one of the most misunderstood emotions. It's often considered ugly and bad and indicative of a failing relationship. It's associated with violence and many go to extreme lengths to avoid it. It can't be avoided, only repressed. Since it's there, we must learn how to make peace with it. Anger can be dealt with constructively, or it can destroy two people. In Chapter 6 we learn how to deal with anger and how to grow from this relationship fact of life.

Chapter 6

Making Peace with Anger

Anger is like our emotional thermometer. It lets us know psychically that things are amiss . . .

Brian Wolfe, MFT
formerly in private practice, San Francisco, CA
(now living in New Zealand)

Being in love creates happiness and emotional fulfillment that is unparalleled. Love also provides nurturance when there's depletion, sanctuary when there's danger, grounding when there's confusion. You are indeed fortunate if you've found the right one, which makes wanting to kill your lover (figuratively) so much more confusing. How can the man who inhabits your soul also infuriate you? How can the guy who creates so much joy be such a royal pain in the ass? The short answer is that you are two complex creatures with a vast array of individual needs. Those needs cannot always be in sync. At times he will say and do things that will get on your nerves—and you will become angry.

Anger comes from pain. Sources of pain are bountiful in intimate relationships because love means emotional vulnerability. What he says and does matters, and when it's not what you want, it will hurt.

Anger is a reaction to pain because it serves, at least temporarily, to mitigate discomfort. If you feel hurt when he's inconsiderate, anger gives you a sense of power and control. "What an insensitive jerk—he isn't getting away with this" feels better than "I don't matter to him."

This is not to say that anger itself is always dysfunctional. On the contrary, acknowledging and appropriately expressing anger is healthy. In the previous example, your anger can motivate you to communi-cate the unacceptability of his behavior, which could cause him to re-

Man Talk: The Gay Couple's Communication Guide
© 2007 by The Haworth Press, Inc. All rights reserved.
doi:10.1300/5527_07

flect and change. Furthermore, regardless of his reaction, letting your lover know what is unacceptable to you via your expression of anger is a form of self-care. One of the biggest mistakes you can make in a relationship is to love someone at the expense of your own well-being. Nevertheless, it can be difficult for you to feel that it's okay to be angry with him. Why?

> In my family if you get angry and say it and really get angry, then that's cause for everyone to withdraw and not talk for a long time.
>
> > Harvey, age 42, physican
> > Cleveland, Ohio

> We are socialized as children to not be angry . . . Our parents would tell us "don't be angry at your sister; you should love her" even though she just clobbered you on the head with your toy truck.
>
> > Brian Wolfe, MFT
> > formerly in private practice, San Francisco, CA
> > (now living in New Zealand)

> I think it's bad [anger]. I don't think people should feel it . . . And when I do feel angry, 'cause it does happen, I don't know what to do with it.
>
> > Aidan, 37, physical therapist
> > Tampa, Florida

Anger Isn't Pretty

Anger is an unpopular emotion. It's considered ugly, distasteful, and something to avoid. There are a number of reasons for this.

> It's ugly and I don't want to show that face.
>
> > Aidan, 37, physical therapist
> > Tampa, Florida

Anger Is Uncomfortable

Anger is not comfortable. It's predicated on pain, and the state of being angry is unpleasant. Expressing anger means you have to deal with conflict and the risks inherent in that action. You or your boyfriend may succumb to raw emotions resulting in a fight that goes no-where. Expressing anger appropriately takes thought, control of emotions, agreement about ground rules and lots of energy. No wonder it's seductive to avoid it.

Anger Isn't "Nice"

We don't like anger because it goes against social edict. Social means being pleasant, agreeable, friendly, accommodating, quiet. Anger is none of that. It removes pleasantries. It takes away a happy or neutral mood and creates overt acrimony. You may avoid expressing anger because you don't want to start trouble or be a killjoy.

> You're not supposed to be angry. People who are angry are "bad." It's an emotion that I think we're taught not to acknowledge.
>
> Simon, 34, attorney
> Madison, Wisconsin

Anger Is Counter-Relationship

Relationship is about love, support, caring, and being on the same side. It's about connection. When you feel angry with him, you feel none of that. Being angry may be something you try to avoid because you feel it has no rightful place in your relationship.

Disconnection

The sense of being disconnected is very threatening. *At that moment* you may question why you're with him or if your love him. You may feel only disgust. Although those feelings generally pass when anger leaves, while you're in the midst of such emotion you may feel that you could never connect again.

Anger Kills Relationships

Couples who are chronically disagreeing are not happy and often do not (and should not!) remain together. Getting angry may feel threatening to your relationship because each time you experience anger you fear it's eroding the good feelings you have with each other. It feels like another nail is being hammered into the coffin. That is accurate if your anger serves as a distraction from unresolved, serious difficulties. For example, you are sexually frustrated but instead of discussing this you are chronically angry about untidiness. This is different from periodic anger that is related to real issues and resolvable. That kind of anger is universal and does not kill a relationship.

Anger Equals Violence

Generally speaking, people in my field make sense. Occasionally, however, someone does not. I once heard a fellow mental health professional say that to be angry is always bad, wrong, no good, and hurtful. He said, "Why do you think they call it *mad*?"

This is particularly scary coming from a professional. But the bigger concern is that it reflects a widespread, irrational supposition. Many of us equate anger with being crazy. Being crazy means being out of control and often violent.

Our world is, in fact, filled with craziness and violence that grows worse with every hour. September 11 was the beginning of the "new normal" that has made violence an in-your-face reality. The unremitting threat of terrorism creates a chronic expectation and fear of bloodshed. But it's not only terrorism. America is plagued with insanity and brutality. Youngsters committing mass murder at school, indiscriminate gang shootings, and child abduction and murders are but a few of the many horrors we face daily. Add to this that scores of us grew up in violent families. Violence is then even more terrifying because it has been a personal life experience.

But this is about violence, not anger—a huge difference. Violence is predicated by anger, but all anger does not lead to violence. In fact, as with other feelings, it you are able to be aware of your anger and address it, the chance of acting it out is decreased.

This is not easy to accept, however. Oftentimes, people have thoughts and images of violence when angry, so they fear that their mental pictures will easily spill into behavior. Their reaction is to immediately stuff the feeling in order to feel safe, but that only creates more anger. This may not cause acting out, but it may grow an ulcer, or it may create bitterness or grudge holding. Avoiding anger simply doesn't work.

When Anger Is Destructive

The opposite pole of the spectrum doesn't work either. Raging will kill a relationship just as swiftly as avoidance will.

The angriest person I ever met with was a young man I knew in my twenties who was in a persistent state of extreme fury. "How are you?" I would say, which would be greeted with "You don't care." He would rant literally for an hour nonstop when I called him, and if I tried to say one word he shot back, "You're interrupting me." When I attempted to empathize with his feelings, he countered with "You don't understand me and you're not listening." When I told him he could drop dead (even at age twenty-five) because he was in such an intense rage, he grew angrier and blamed his potential death on me. No one in the world could do right by him; no one in the world ever did right by him. He was too poor, his boss was out to get him, the New York City air was poison, and girls didn't like him because they were all snobs. Bus drivers were all nasty, taxi drivers were too stupid, restaurants were dirty and waiters spread diseases. His tooth ached, his arm was swollen but doctors and dentists were only out for money. He was depressed, couldn't sleep, couldn't enjoy anything, but therapists did nothing but talk and steal your money. And he wasn't responsible for any of his misery, according to him.

This, of course, is an extreme example of injurious anger. It's instructive, nevertheless, because it exemplifies the dynamics of the problem in bold relief. Destructive anger is chronic, at the wrong source(s), at the imperfect, excessive, paranoid, unable to take any responsibility for one's pain anger, and anger that isolates you from others. We will now examine these and some other dynamics of destructive anger on the next few pages.

Becoming Aware of the Problem

Getting a handle on this begins by recognizing that your anger is excessive and problematic. There is much in this world to be angry about. Large city environmental stresses, miserable jobs, the state of the world and your moody boyfriend are all legitimate reasons to be angry. Volumes could be written on the multitudinous ways life can piss all of us off.

But if you find yourself in a chronic state of anger, something is not working. You can't be angry all the time because you're poisoning your life. Ask yourself this: How often and how intensely angry am I? I don't have a magic scale to define "too much," but if you find you're angry a good deal of your wakening hours, you have a problem. It's a judgment call, but if you're questioning it, it's probably too much.

You may think that nothing is wrong but others may be telling you that you're too angry and need to "calm down." Listen. Sometimes we are so angry that it's hard to reflect and realize that the anger itself is the issue. You may be too caught up in the individual issues that are enraging you to see the larger problem of your anger.

If your anger is across the spectrum of your life, I suggest you consult with a therapist or an anger management program. Something is going on underneath your skin that needs to be addressed. The external environment, as provoking as it can be, is the not the primary issue.

Destructive Anger in Your Relationship

While anger and disagreements are normal in any relationship, this should not *define* your relationship. Your relationship should be, *for the most part,* an area in life in which peace and support and good feelings abound. The relationship should create an emotional space that decreases stress, not causes it. Going home should provide a safe haven from the difficulties of the world. You shouldn't be leaving home to escape the difficulties of your relationship. You should also consider how anger and disagreements manifest between you and your partner. Do you have big explosions that last for days? Do you hold on to anger? Do your disagreements end with a feeling that nothing was solved? Do you have a persistent feeling of anger toward your lover? Do you ever become violent?

All of these are signs that point to destructive anger. Violence is in a category of its own which I'll address at the end of this section.

What Causes Destructive Anger?

Family Modeling

How anger was managed in your family of origin will play an enormous role in your behavior. Suppose your dad barked whenever he was frustrated. Suppose also that he got his needs met when he did this. If you were there, what do you think you would have learned?

This was Gavin's experience. Born in the mid-fifties to a lower middle class family in Philadelphia, Gavin's father was a laborer who started his day at 5 a.m. because it took him two hours to get to work. When he returned in the evening he was not a happy camper, and everything had to be "right" or there would be hell to pay. He would first demand of his wife, Ursula, to bring him a cold beer and a snack. If the beer didn't come fast enough he screamed and cursed, "Get the fucking beer for Christ's sakes! Don't I work hard enough around here to get a little respect?" Out came Ursula flying with the beer and food. If the beer, God forbid, was not cold enough, he would fling it against the wall, along with the food. Ursula *would apologize,* run to get him another beer, and pray that this one was colder. She would then wipe up the mess he made.

Gavin was able to look back at this and recognize that his father was abusive. He held a great deal of anger toward this man for his behavior. He did not want to be like his father. But unfortunately, he was.

When he asked a question of his boyfriend Luis and Luis didn't answer him fast enough, out came "I asked you a question, you deaf asshole. What's wrong with you?" When his computer crashed one morning as he was trying to pay a bill online, he kicked the computer so hard that he broke the hard drive. When he felt ill and Luis tried to comfort him, the warmth of Luis's hand made him more uncomfortable because he had a fever. So he screamed "Get your fucking hand off me, asshole. Don't you see I'm sick?"

While we may not like what our parents did, we often find ourselves saying and doing exactly what they said and did. Why? Because we learn from demonstration. Living under the same roof in such a significant relationship as one with a parent(s) provides a powerful education (for better or for worse) on how to deal with many things, including anger.

Adding to Gavin's experience was that the behavior worked. Dad screamed and Mom brought the beer. Dad threw the beer (and food) and Mom cleaned it up. Gavin learned this connection even though on a conscious level he abhorred such behavior. When his emotional trigger (frustration) was activated, out came anger management from 1956!

One strategy for overcoming this is to reflect on the ways your parents behaved (or currently behave) toward each other. Try to uncover the similarities in your behavior, particularly in relation to your lover. You may discover, perhaps to your horror, that although the issues and words are different, much is the same MO. This realization is the first step in changing your behavior. The next step is to make a conscious effort to become aware of it and control it. Although this will not be easy to do, with practice it can be achieved. We're affected, but not controlled, by our history.

The Explosion/Relief Myth

Many people believe that letting it all out relieves the pressure of anger. It's a myth supported by images of therapists guiding their clients to hit pillows or and/or scream out their anger. Studies show the contrary, however.[1] Not only does raging not relieve pressure, it makes you more angry. Furthermore, it solves nothing. You're unable to have a rational conversation while raging.

Positive Reinforcement

Having an emotional explosion can provide one advantage; you may achieve instant gratification. Your boyfriend speaks the wrong words, you scream "shut up," and he does. In an instant you've garnered a sense of control and relief. This was the scenario with Gavin's father and mother. But your relief may be short-lived. That kind of behavior stifles communication and is likely to create resentment in your partner. Eventually, or perhaps sooner, he may come back at you with his own emotional explosion that can create an out-of-control confrontation.

Not Letting Go

Some folks resist getting over anger. Holding on is a form of power. As long as they're angry, they're in charge, or so they think. They maintain a sense of entitlement and being "owed." Moreover,

---

[1]McKay, Judith, McKay, Matthew, and Rogers, Peter D, *When Anger Hurts—Quieting The Storm Within,* Oakland, California: New Harbinger Publications, Inc., 1989, pp. 18-22.

there's no need to do the complex work of negotiating, forgiving, and moving on. Holding on to anger creates a simplified world of black-and-white where the angry person is right and the other person is wrong.

Not only is this the antithesis of problem solving, but it keeps anger at the surface, ready to spring forth without much provocation. This can easily incite one's partner into an irate reaction, fueling more anger, and making communication and problem solving increasingly elusive.

Holding on to anger can also be a form of passive-aggressive behavior. "Nothing is wrong," you bellow out as you smirk and remain uncharacteristically silent. This then provokes your lover into playing the guessing game of "what is really wrong?" As you continue to deny a problem, his stress level rises and both of you proceed to go nowhere. Except to get angrier at each other.

When you're initially provoked, it 's not easy to *immediately* let go because you're physiologically aroused and have anger inciting thoughts and images. That is normal in the moment. It can be okay for a few hours, but not for a few days. People who don't let go, keep anger-inciting thoughts and images alive. Over and over again they ruminate about how they've been wronged, how horrible it has been, and how they're not going to let their partner get away with it.

Letting go means making a conscious effort to change this thinking. It means buying into the fact that staying angry will hurt *you*. When you're holding on to anger you can't be feeling good. It also means recognizing that such rumination keeps one a legendary victim only in one's mind. The sense of power and entitlement that you have is really an illusion. Your partner is likely to think that you're being unreasonable and further apologies and "making up" may be the last thing he desires or is even capable of delivering. You, the holding on person, are not going to feel vindicated as your lover doesn't offer additional requests for forgiveness. You will probably experience more feelings of victimization and discontent.

Physical Discomfort

Feeling tired, having a pain in your back, or beginning to come down with a cold is not a reason to be angry with your partner, yet when we're in a physically uncomfortable state, we're more sensitive to anything that annoys us. When you're feeling healthy and alert a less than well-thought-out comment by your partner may go unnoticed. When you're not feeling well you may tell him to "shut up." Obviously, starting an altercation with him will not improve your physical comfort.

The best way to handle this is to realize that when you're physically uncomfortable, you're more likely to strike out inappropriately. Just the knowledge of this and the will to control it can prevent a problem.

It's also not a bad a idea to serve notice to your partner that you're not feeling well or tired and to request that he be a little more sensitive to how you feel. It's legitimate at times like this to say, "I would like a little silence" or "I'd like to be left alone for now" or "I don't feel up to discussing anything important right now." This can avert a wholly needless problem from materializing.

Imperfection

All of us are flawed human beings. When you're with someone, especially for a long period, you will bear witness to many imperfections. When he forgets to throw out the garbage, when he says and does the wrong thing, when he's embarrassing and stupid, you're not going to be immune to your feelings. But if you get bent out of shape every time he makes a mistake, you're going to look like a pretzel. You need to embrace the larger picture of human fallibility. You need to make peace with that within yourself and in relation to him, otherwise, you're going to have chronic anger that can't be resolved.

Depression

Depressed people are angry people. Freud described depression as anger tuned inward, but depressed people can certainly turn it outward also. Irritability is part of the clinical picture of depression.

If you or your partner or both of you are depressed, you need expert help with this. The good news is that there are many treatments for depression. The bad news is that untreated depression can be a threat not only to your relationship but to your survival.

Anger secondary to depression is unhealthy and will not remit unless the depression is lifted. If you have any concern about this, seek a competent mental health professional or speak to your family physician.

False Victimization

If you feel victimized, you will be angry. Being a victim means you have been harmed, and that you have neither responsibility nor control over what ensued. If you're waiting in line in a bank, and you're taken hostage during a robbery, you're a victim. If you go to your mother-in-law's home for Mother's Day when you didn't want to, you're not a victim. Scores of us don't see it that way, however.

We think we can't say no, and then resent those who "made" us do what we didn't want to do. This is a significant reason for chronic destructive anger in relationships.

Relationships are about compromise, which means that you have to find a balance in how you conduct your life with your lover. You don't have the unfettered freedom that you have when you're single. But compromise, which means not always getting your first choice, means *that you can live with the choice you agree to.*

This is always a judgment call, and there is no "right" or "wrong" nor could there be any universal agreement on what is okay or not okay for *you.* I may consider it a mild inconvenience to go to dinner with my partner and a friend of his whom I don't like. You may consider it torture to have dinner with someone you don't like. We make ourselves victims in many ways.

Inability to Recognize Your Needs

Saying "no" is extremely difficult for some. First, saying no implies that you recognize what you can't tolerate. Those of us raised in homes where our needs were seldom validated have real difficulty actually knowing what is okay and what isn't. You may engage in behavior that you discover is not acceptable only when you're in the midst of it. It then becomes easy to point a finger at the person who "made" you do it, rather than acknowledging the confusing and complex problem you have with understanding your own needs.

Delegitimizing Your Needs

Saying no means not only understanding your needs but feeling it's okay to have them. If, as, in the previous example, your partner tells you that your sense of torture is an overreaction, and you go along with this, you are invalidating your own needs. I want to emphasize *you are invalidating your needs. Not him.* No one but you can decide what is acceptable for you. Certainly you may not appreciate his lack of support, but if anger becomes directed at him, you're distracting yourself. You're missing the point that you're letting someone else decide for you what is and isn't okay. *That's your issue, not his.*

This doesn't mean that you can't be flexible and be able to make peace with something you thought you couldn't. But be aware that if you have a history of abdicating your needs, you are at much higher risk of accepting the unacceptable than of being inflexible. This is confusing and sometimes therapy is needed to untangle the confusion.

Lack of Boundaries

Boundaries are emotional lines in the sand. The help us recognize the division between our needs and those around us. Boundaries are sometimes thought of as a way to close ourselves off from others and be "selfish," which is a distortion of what healthy boundaries are about. Being closed means not growing. Healthy boundaries imply an open system. You consider others and are considerate of them. You can and need to be accommodating, but you don't lose sight of the separation of needs. You don't negotiate the non-negotiable. You don't give away the farm.

When we have problems with boundaries, we confuse our needs with others. We strive to meet other's needs at the expense of our own. This is unhealthy in every sense of the word. A colleague of mine once commented that there's a blurry line between "being nice to others" and self-destructiveness. I agree. I'm not saying you shouldn't be good to your fellow person, just don't destroy yourself in the process.

Sometimes having little or no boundaries can be life threatening. The following conversation took place between a client (Peter) and his therapist. Peter is a forty-seven-year-old, bright, successful businessman in Dayton, Ohio.

PETER: I'm embarrassed to say this . . . but he fucked me up the ass without a condom.

THERAPIST: Tell me what happened.

PETER: He mounted me from behind. I kind of knew what was coming.

THERAPIST: What did you know was coming?

PETER: I knew he didn't have a condom on. They were on the night table. I asked him to put it on but he refused. I knew he was going to enter me when he got on top of me.

THERAPIST: Did you want him to fuck you without a condom?

PETER: Are you crazy? Absolutely not! I was totally turned off. I didn't even have a hard on.

THERAPIST: Why didn't you tell him to stop?

PETER: Don't know . . . Well, he was really into it. I would have messed up his fun.

THERAPIST: But you didn't want him to do it? Correct?

PETER: Correct.

THERAPIST: Then why did you let him do it?

PETER: Well . . . I thought he would have enough sense to use a condom. That's why I put them on the table.

THERAPIST: But he didn't use them. You knew that. And you knew it while he was entering you. Did he force you?

PETER: Oh, no way. He's a pretty nice guy. He would have jumped back in a heartbeat if I said no.

THERAPIST: Then why didn't you say no?

PETER: Not sure. Guess it would have ruined the moment for him. He would have thought I was a wet rag.

THERAPIST: So you let him do something you didn't want him to do, something potentially dangerous to you?

PETER: Yeah, and now I'm worried. I know he runs around a lot. And if he did this with me he's probably doing this with others. He's probably positive. And I'm not. At least maybe until now. I felt so disgusted in his shower. I was wiping the cum out of my ass and I just wanted to kill him. He fell asleep. I left without saying goodbye. What a fucking bastard he is. I never want to see him again.

Take note of how he externalizes the problem. His anger at the man who fucked him without a condom is his way of avoiding recognition that he had a choice. This is how he perpetuates his sense of having no boundaries and being a victim.

Even in much less extreme situations, having healthy boundaries is essential. Lack of adequate boundaries creates caregiving for those who don't need it and in the process stifles their individuality. When you're in someone's head more than your own, you're doing for them what they can and should be doing for themselves. You're also abdicating your own needs, which creates anger because you are in fact being violated. "Self" violated, for sure, but violated nevertheless. It also produces expectations that can't be met. If you live your life for others, you want payback. When you don't get it, you'll be even angrier.

Intimate, loving relationships test the ability to have healthy boundaries because you love your man and understandably want to do everything you can to make him happy. So how do you know when you've crossed the line? When are you so involved with your lover's needs that you lose sight of your own?

This is complicated, but one clue is a definitive warning sign. If your care for him is beginning to *hurt,* you're over the line. The hurt comes from the intention to *make and make is impossible to do*. You can support, enhance, and color his happiness and his life. But you can't *make* him happy. You can't rescue him. You can't *give* him a life. He has the responsibility for that. When you try that, you're embarking on mission impossible which will compromise your own needs.

Pay *very close attention* to that feeling of hurt even it is ever so faint. If it's there, it's growing, and it will develop into anger that will ultimately injure both of you.

Fear of Conflict

Dealing directly with a discordant situation can be frightening for those who live by avoidance. Putting the naked "no" on the table eliminates smoke and mirrors. "No, I don't want to go out with you again," "No, I will have not have sex with you now," "No, this relationship is not working" is unambiguous. The expression, "What part of no don't you understand?" comes to mind. This is clear, no wasting of time, healthy communication, but it invites a reaction.

Some will do anything to keep away from that reaction. In their minds ambiguity protects them for another day when they can figure out yet another way to avoid the reaction, or just hope the person will go away. Avoidance is safety. Being direct is dangerous. Or so they think.

To be direct in an inharmonious situation means there's a fairly good chance the other person will be disappointed, unhappy, unsatisfied, and even angry, maybe very angry. This is terrifying for some.

Fear of conflict is related to a host of issues including delegitimization of one's needs, low self-esteem, boundary problems, and dysfunctional family modeling of conflict. The primary dynamic, however, for conflict avoiders is a deep sense of vulnerability. It comes down to "I will make him mad and he will hurt me."

Stan and Alex are good friends. Stan has had a couple of dates with Harry, a man he met at professional conference. Both are engineers and live in Chicago. Harry is obnoxious; he's loud, rude, and everything Stan finds unacceptable. After their second date Stan swore he would not go out with him again. The following is a conversation Stan had with his friend Alex.

STAN: I probably shouldn't tell you this. But guess who I'm meeting for coffee Saturday afternoon?

ALEX: Please don't tell me it's that guy, Harry.

STAN: Yeah.

ALEX: Are you crazy?

STAN: What?

ALEX: You told me he bores you to tears. That he's a jerk. That he's pompous and that he has legs that look like tree stumps. You swore just last week you'd never see him again.

STAN: Oh, I don't care.

ALEX: What do you mean you "don't care"? You told me *you can't stand the guy.*

STAN: But he called.

ALEX: So?

STAN: So it's just coffee. It won't take that long.

ALEX: But you don't like him. You ranted about how you can't stand him. Do I have a hearing problem, a memory problem, or am I delusional?

STAN: No. I did say that.

ALEX: Then why would you consider having coffee with this man again? Why would you consider spending two seconds with someone you don't like?

STAN: But Alex, maybe he won't confirm. He has to call by tomorrow night.

ALEX: Are you deaf?

STAN: What?

ALEX: Don't be cute with me. Why are you doing this?

STAN: I don't know . . . Well, he's in my field. It's a small professional community. He could make trouble.

ALEX: Trouble?

STAN: You know, if I get him angry, he may talk. He may say bad things about me. Who knows how that could affect me the next time I look for a job?

ALEX: Stan, you know I love you and I've been your friend for over ten years. But you're out of your mind and you need therapy.

STAN: No, I don't. Maybe he won't call.

ALEX: You need therapy and I need a drink. As I said, I love you but this conversation is over.

Distrust

Trust is a principal component of intimacy. Without it there's no relationship. Trust is not a given and needs to be earned, but some of us cannot trust no matter how trustworthy our partner is. Problems with trust can be deep seated and related to traumatic experiences in childhood. They can also be related to traumatic experiences in adulthood. If someone you loved has deceived you, it can very difficult to feel safe with someone else.

Distrusting your lover means you are chronically on guard and ready to be deceived. You can't feel good toward him in such a state. You're likely to have unremitting feelings of anger. He is likely to feel the same toward you because his experience is that of being unfairly suspect and accused.

Domestic Violence

Domestic violence may have some or all of the above elements of inappropriate anger. But domestic violence is *violence,* not just anger. If you are being hit in any way, threatened with your physical safety, or feeling emotionally abused, or if you engage in abusive behavior, *you need professional help immediately.* I don't see this as a good idea. I view this as an *imperative,* which can even make the difference between life and death. Help must come from someone who has expertise in gay domestic violence.

How to Express Anger Appropriately

This process of handling anger constructively with your partner begins with speaking to the issues described in this chapter. If you want a man in your life, you're going to have to reconcile that anger is a relationship reality. Being willing to accept conflict, refusing to be a false victim, controlling emotional explosiveness, unlearning the dysfunctional lessons of your family, and having good boundaries are among the requisites. That being said, how do you go about finding a resolution when you're legitimately angry with him? What do you say and do that will get you to the place where your anger is dispelled as the source of it is addressed and transformed?

Chose Your Battles

Although I've made the argument that avoidance of problems solves nothing, this doesn't mean that you need to discuss every crinkle in your relationship. All of us are flawed, and if you've discussed everything that wasn't perfect about him, that's all you'd be doing. It's a judgment call, but minor issues that mildly annoy you may be best left alone.

Ground Rules

Before either of you can address angry feelings, you need to have rules about how you do this. Why? Because when you're angry your emotions can drive the bus. That's never a good idea. Raw, angry emotion can escalate rather quickly and obliterate communication. Rules decided before you're angry can help prevent that. For example, you may decide that yelling, name-calling, or any other form of personal attacking is unacceptable.

Time and Space for Anger

Each man in a couple should have the opportunity to be heard. A simple request to talk should be honored without question. It's highly destructive to respond with "Oh, you're angry again. I don't have time for this," because it de-legitimizes the person's feelings. Thus, you should have an agreement that if either one of you feels the need to talk about something that made you angry, the opportunity to do so is not debatable.

When and Where to Talk

If you're extremely upset, it's best to wait until you cool down before you talk. It may feel counterintuitive to do this because your anger begs for a resolution. However, the emotional fire may simply make it impossible to have a rational discussion. Set a time (not too far in the future—perhaps in a couple of hours) when you can talk.

You should not be distracted when you discuss anger. Cell phones, landlines, and pagers should be turned off. The TV should be off. Appointments should not be scheduled close to this time because you don't want to feel you have to end the discussion prematurely.

Drinking or using other kinds of mind-altering drugs needs to be avoided. You require a clear head and good control of your rational, problem-solving capabilities.

You need privacy during this time. Restaurants and other public places will not work. If you don't live together and one of you has a roommate, he or she shouldn't be around during this time. Sometimes just knowing another person is in the house can stifle your discussion. Obviously, you can't throw your roommate out if he lives there. Do the best you can, but the more private, the better.

Before going to sleep, before going to work, or before one of you leaves for a trip are not good times to have a conversation involving anger. Again, you may feel pressed to get the problem resolved quickly but those factors can make resolution elusive. Discussions involving anger are not necessarily solved in one conversation, and may even exacerbate discomfort initially. You don't want your sleep, workday, or trip messed up. That will only add another issue of contention.

Of course, spontaneous discussions when you're angry will and should take place. You don't have to plan to have a talk; just make sure the above criteria are met.

Being in the Wrong Place at the Wrong Time

But what if you can't meet those criteria? What if you're in a situation where you can't have a serious discussion and you can't get away from each other? Perhaps you're together in a car, or you're in a restaurant away from home on a trip, or with friends. You've become very angry, you can't stand what he just said, and there he is next to you. What do you do?

This is a time when you need to temporarily avoid a discussion. You must quickly close down any attempt at conversation. This is not the right place and time, and if you try to talk it will backfire. A serious conversation while driving can cause an accident. A discussion in public or in front of friends can be very embarrassing and may cause new problems.

I recommend proceeding with the following three steps. They should be agreed upon in advance.

1. *Refrain*—No matter how counterintuitive this feels, cease and desist from saying anything further about the matter. Don't try to get in a last shot. You want to prevent the situation from escalating and the best thing to do is stop the discussion dead in its tracks. Either one of you can initiate this by simply saying, "this is for later." If you agree upon this phase or something like it in advance, both of you will know what to do once it is said. After this is done, remain silent with each other for a while. At a moment when you are angry and confined, you may be close to an explosion. Anything said could be a trigger for that.

2. *Distract*—Anger, as anxiety, can de-escalate with distraction. As you focus on something else, your mind moves away from rage-producing thoughts. You're literally replacing those thoughts with different ones. Within a short time your anger can significantly decrease. Even if this feels artificial, do it anyway. You'll be amazed at the change in physiological arousal.

If you're with friends, you may want to talk with one of them about a topic that would normally interest you, but you can focus on anything as a distraction. People who have anxiety attacks may find it helpful to notice the colors in their environment, or observe shapes of objects, or study the formation of clouds. You can do the same with anger. If you're in a restaurant, for example, observe the shape and size of your table, look at the colors and patterns of the dishes, observe the lighting on the walls. This may seem mindless but it's not. The point is to force yourself to focus on something else, whatever that is, in order to take you mind away from rumination and escalation. It does work.

3. *Re-enter*—Once the initial flush of anger has passed and you're feeling calmer, go back to whatever you were doing. I call this "re-entering." Obviously, the issue of contention is still there, but it's off the table until you're in a more suitable environment to deal with it.

I'm not referring to a weighty issue where anger could be extreme (e.g., you just learned that he's having an affair). The best thing in such a situation would be to continue not to interact or if necessary, leave the environment. Re-entering can take place when you still have anger but it's of a less serious nature.

But you may say, "Okay, I don't to want to scream anymore, but I'm still angry. Why should I act as if I'm not?"

I'm not asking you to act. I'm asking you to put the anger somewhere else temporarily, so you can get on with whatever you were doing. I recognize that this will be difficult, if not impossible for some. But consider this: Sometimes we give anger much more power than it ought to have. When we have anger, we convince ourselves that we must behave in a certain way, that we can't be "nice" or loving because we're angry. That's more of a self-fulfilling prophecy than anything else. Your lover is much more than the thing he said or did that irritated you. He's the guy you love, your one and only. If you keep that in mind it will be easier to feel loving and relaxed. When you can let go, even if the issue is not yet resolved, you send a message to yourself and your partner that you're still a devoted couple, that the anger doesn't change who you are, and that you're stronger than the anger. Furthermore, by not re-entering, you destroy the present, which you will never have again. The trip you are on, the day out with friends, or the dinner you are having is never going to be repeated exactly the same way. Don't lose the present.

Disrespect

Disrespect is a deal breaker. No one is going to feel comfortable or motivated to problem solve if he is being disrespected in the process.

Respect means listening and avoiding any behavior that denigrates what the other person is saying. You should have an agreement that when one person speaks the other doesn't interrupt. There should be no stopwatch. "Okay, you're just blabbing now; finish what you're saying" is quite disrespectful. I'm not advocating filibusters or monologues but each person needs the time to say what he wants to say. He decides the time, not you.

Doing something else while your partner is talking is also disrespectful. No, you can't do two things at the same time, and even if you could, that is a nonverbal communication of impertinence. You need each other's *undivided* attention.

Making faces, rolling your eyes, or sighing also conveys invalidation of what your partner is saying. I'm not expecting you to sit there like a robot, but it's imperative that you be aware of your body language. Nonverbal gestures are powerful and can stifle communication even faster than saying "shut up."

Some people feel their anger somehow gives them license to be nasty. It doesn't, and all it will do is stop the process of problem solving dead in its tracks.

Listening to Understand

In Chapter 7 we will explore in detail the process of listening. At this juncture listening doesn't mean sitting there planning your strategy of response. It means hearing his point of view and trying your best to appreciate his frame of reference. Listening doesn't mean agreeing necessarily. It means endeavoring to understand.

One exercise you may experiment with is to watch someone on TV with whom you have a diametrically opposed point of view. Watch him or her say what you believe is ridiculous, wrong, stupid, immoral, and horrible. Antigay folks work well for me! The more this person's view bothers you, the better. Then put your emotions in a corner and try to *understand* where he's coming from. Ask yourself what's he seeing, thinking, fearful of, angry about, distrustful of, etc. You can still hate and disagree with him and wish he took a one-way rocket ship to Pluto. But try to *understand* him.

When you do this with your partner you open up a whole new world for yourself. You can discover that he's not really out of his mind but that he simply has a different viewpoint. Understanding another's point of view can become the first step toward finding a middle ground.

Reflective Listening

One way to help understand what your partner is trying to communicate is to reflect back *your understanding* of what he's saying. If you're wrong he can try to correct you. If you're right, you're not only getting it, but you're letting him know you are getting it. Again, this doesn't mean you're agreeing with him, just trying to understand his point of view. In the process, however, you may soften your position.

This is an excellent way to decrease anger, find a middle ground and build intimacy. Nothing is more relationship enhancing than knowing you're being heard and understood by your partner. The following vignette illustrates this process.

Abe and Gene are a couple in their late twenties living in Portland, Oregon. Abe is a social worker and Gene is a teacher. They were at a party hosted by a colleague of Gene's on a Saturday evening in the fall. A number of teachers attended, including a teacher who had been transferred out of Gene's school a year previously. Gene had been friendly with this man (Bob) but hadn't spoken to him or seen him since. They had a lot of catching up to do. As a result, he spent most of the evening talking with Bob. Abe felt ignored. He also found Bob attractive and was certain there was some sexual tension going on between Bob and Gene. As the night progressed he felt more out of sorts and wound up sitting by himself getting drunk. When he left with Gene, he was very angry. Gene apologized for spending so much time with Bob but it didn't change anything. Abe said, "Please just drive; I don't want to talk now." Gene complied. When they reached their home, Abe said nothing, pulled out an extra blanket and pillow from the closet, and went to sleep by himself on the couch downstairs. The next morning he was ready to talk and Gene was ready to listen. The following conversation ensued:

ABE: I am very angry with you. That was really bad last night. I had to sit all alone while you spent the whole damn evening with that guy, Bob.

GENE: We had a lot of catching up to do. But you're right. I got carried away with it. I was rude not only to you but to the others.

ABE: Look, I don't give a shit about the others. I'm your lover and you simply ignored me while you flirted with pretty boy. That sucks.

GENE: Flirted?

ABE: Yes, flirted.

GENE: Hmm . . .

ABE: I hardly knew anyone there. I was sitting alone for more than two hours, like a pathetic schmuck. Others saw me by myself and you were over there with Bob and everybody knows you're my lover. Everyone was giving me polite smiles but I knew what they were thinking. How do you think that made me feel? I wanted the floor to just open up and swallow me. And could I get out of there? No. Because we came in one car. So to say anything to you would have just made a scene. What a fucked up night I had.

GENE: So let me see if I understand this. You're saying that not only did you feel I was rude by ignoring you, and not only were you irritated by what seemed to you like flirting, but that I was also humiliating you?

ABE: You hit it right on the head.

GENE: And to top that, you felt trapped because we came with one car?

ABE: Bingo.

GENE: I really do see how you could feel horrible.

The discussion is not over at this point, but they're well on their way to finding a resolution. Abe can see that Gene truly understands what he went through that night and that is half of the battle. Note that Gene didn't see himself as flirting but rather as catching up with a former colleague. He may even think that Abe's perception of everyone watching them is in his head, but he doesn't say that. He's reflecting what he *understands to be Abe's emotional experience* because that's what's needed to communicate *understanding*. He may at some point clarify that he wasn't flirting and that his familiarity with his colleagues makes it unlikely that they were thinking what Abe believed they were thinking. But that could come only after he communicates that he understands where Abe is coming from.

Yelling

My father was a yeller: Little came out of his mouth that wasn't three times the normal decibels required. If he was annoyed with my mom, he yelled. If he was angry with me, he yelled. He talked about his boss Ralph, whom he hated, and he yelled.

In the earlier days of my childhood, I was truly curious as to why he did this. Did he think we heard him better when he sounded like a megaphone? Did he think we were deaf? What was his purpose?

These were well-founded questions, even though they came from my immature mind. There was no rational purpose to his yelling. We weren't deaf and the only thing he accomplished was to have all of us walk on eggshells. Or yell back.

During a conversation that involves anger, it's easy to escalate as the anger-causing issues come to the forefront. Raising your voice is indicative of escalation, but it also tends to cause escalation. Yelling will accomplish nothing other than putting your lover on the defensive, getting you even angrier, and possibly degenerating the discussion into a screaming match. And you may come out it hoarse to boot! Remaining calm is much easier said than done, however. Thus, it's imperative to plan ahead.

Anger Scale

In order to remain calm, you can do a number of things. As you speak, make a mental note of your anger level. Make a scale going from one to ten. One means you're as calm as a Valium, ten you're screaming out of control and have lost the ability to communicate. Obviously, you want to stay as far away from ten as possible.

As you're feeling irritated, do some internal assessing. Are you at a three, close to a four? Are you past five? You rating is, of course, subjective, but that's fine. If you feel you're at a seven, you're pissed, and that's important for you to know. You can even make yourself a little business card–sized scale. Draw a line from one to ten. Color the lower numbers in decreasing shades of blue as they increase. At number five, begin coloring the numbers in increasing shades of red. You can refer to this if it's easier than doing it in your head.

The purpose of this is to make you very aware of your anger so that you can do something about it before it's too late. As we become irate, we focus intensely on the anger-causing thoughts and images and lose sight of how we are behaving. That's why we can find ourselves suddenly screaming out of control without knowing how we got there. This task makes you pay attention to your behavior and gives you options before you reach the point of no return. When you're at an eight or a ten, you're already screaming, the damage has been done, and it's extremely difficult to back down.

Breathing

One thing you can do as you see yourself going up the scale is to control your breathing. Slow, deep, abdominal breathing decreases anxiety and anger. Since you're always breathing no matter what you do, it's not like you have to take on a whole new activity! Just pay attention to your breathing and begin to take *slow, deep abdominal breaths*. A plethora of books are available on the market that teach relaxation, so pick one up if you need help in learning how to do this.

Paying attention to your breathing will also momentarily distract you from your anger thoughts and images, which can also serve to decrease your anger.

Thoughts and Mental Pictures

As I've indicated previously, *what* you're thinking significantly impacts how you feel. As you escalate in anger, you're thoughts race about, screaming about the sins he committed against you, how it's not fair, how he's gotten away with much too much, and how you're going to let him have it. You're probably also having mental imagery involving the same themes. You "see" him doing what is wrong; you observe the other infractions he committed against you, etc.

If your relationship is worth it, you have other thoughts and images about him that are very satisfying. It may be the time he surprised you on your birthday, or the times that you have had good talks, or the times he was there when you needed him. Before you're in any altercation with your partner, think about those times. Decide which one(s) you can use when you're angry, *then use them.* Certainly this will take some effort. When you're angry, raging thoughts and images dominate and it may feel ridiculous to have anything else. That doesn't mean you can't replace them, however! The other images are also real (probably more accurate) and since you decided what you're going to use beforehand, just put them there. You will not erase your anger in a second, but it can neutralize some of the mental experience of anger that you're having.

Time-Out

Occasionally, no matter how much you plan ahead and intend to remain calm, you cannot. This doesn't mean you have to lose control. You can walk away and stop the process at once. If you leave, the source of your anger is no longer in front of you, and you are therefore likely to calm down. Furthermore, you prevent saying and doing things that you'll regret.

Walking away to prevent an explosion is different from walking away because you're uncomfortable and don't want to deal with him. It's vastly dissimilar from leaving as a means to stick it to him. That can be as destructive as screaming.

A time-out is a way to prevent escalation that will reduce your discussion into meaningless raging. *It's an act of respect and a statement that communication is paramount. Time-out means you come back, and you come back soon to continue your discussion.*

Having a time-out is an agreement you make with your lover *before* you're angry. It says either one of you can leave a discussion temporarily if you feel too angry to continue. You agree to be honest about this and not leave for any other reason (as the ones referred to previously). Either one of you can decide this unilaterally and there is no debate. You agree on a hand signal or simply the phase "time-out." *Once this is executed all speech is stopped in midsentence and both of you physically leave. No last parting shots.* You can go into another room but it's better to leave the house and take a walk. Both of you can leave but obviously not together. Taking a walk is better than going to another room because exercise aids in the deescalation process.

The salient part of the agreement is *that you part for a specific, limited period and then come back.* That's what makes it a respectful process with the aim of problem solving as opposed to avoidance. This is a time- out, a break, not an end to the discussion. You and your lover should decide how long you should be apart, but I wouldn't recommend more than an hour.

During this time don't call a friend on your cell phone to bitch about your lover. This may serve to make you angrier. Make an active attempt to calm down with deep breathing, and visualizing and thinking about something that makes you feel serene (if you relaxed on a recent trip to the mountains, for example, try to picture that event and remember how it felt). You may want to think of nothing or look a objects in your environment that distract you from your anger (an interesting store front, the height of the trees, someone walking her dog, etc.) *Make every effort not to relive the discussion you were just having and that goes double for thinking about how wrong, bad, off the wall, inconsiderate, etc., your lover is.* That is highly destructive rumination that will escalate, not de-escalate you. You should also *not* think of a better strategy to talk with him. While my advice may feel counterintuitive, your only goal in a time-out is to calm down. If you're calm when you get back, you're in the best position to have a rational conversation.

If after you come back you feel you need another time-out, execute it. Take twice the amount of time to come back. Carry it out in the same manner as indicated in the previous paragraph. If you come back and once again either one or both of you feels too angry to negotiate, postpone the discussion for the following day. Again, this can be a unilateral decision and all talk ceases as soon as the hand signal or time out statement is made. In the next twenty-four hours, try to stay away from each other (if you don't live together, do not see each other) and under no circumstances bring up the topic until the next day.

If you feel you need a time out when you begin again on the next day, then it's likely you're going to need a third party to help you with this. That is the next step. "Forgetting about the whole thing" will not work. If this issue has been so difficult that you haven't be able to solve it on you own, it won't go away, and it's likely to tear at your relationship.

Time-out takes time, maybe a lot of it. Not having enough time to do this may mean you don't have enough time for your relationship. Communication is vital to the health of your relationship, and if you need the time-outs so that you can communicate, you need them.

Violation of the rules I presented and which both of you agree to can make the whole process a joke. Coming back to the table means coming back to the table. One hour away is one hour away. Being able to unilaterally end a discussion without parting insults means just that. I highly suggest that after you agree to these rules you write them out and both sign the paper. It's not a bad idea to place this paper in an area where you can both easily see it. If you don't live together, the agreements should be easily available in either of your homes.

Listening Revisited

One of the most vital aspects of communication is the capacity to listen. Listening is not "hearing." True listening means you are able to suspend self-focus as you make every effort to appreciate on a deep level what the other person is experiencing, It not only means understanding his words, but reading his emotions and being able to place yourself, at least temporarily, under his skin. When you succeed at this and are able to let your partner know it, you have made titanic gains toward intimacy. Nothing feels better, nothing brings two people closer together than the mutual appreciation of being heard and understood.

This is not a simple course of action. Active listening takes work and practice, but it can be achieved. We've already begun talking about it. In the next chapter we explore this essential communication tool in more depth.

Chapter 7

Silence and the Art of Listening

Listening is not what you do while you're waiting to talk again.

Brian Wolfe, MFT
formerly in private practice, San Francisco, CA
(now living in New Zealand)

JORDAN: I really don't want to go to Rome. Why don't we spend the week in Chicago? I don't feel comfortable traveling out of the United States right now. With all the craziness going on and all the anti-American stuff, I just won't be able to enjoy it. Every time I see those maniacs hold someone hostage, I'm terrified. I know it's not happening in Italy, but I'm just not comfortable traveling abroad.

CHARLIE: Did you get your passport renewed yet?

JORDAN: Have you heard one word I've said?

CHARLIE: Of course I have. You're just being an idiot.

Charlie is not lying. He heard what Jordan said. But he hadn't been listening. If he were listening, he would appreciate Jordan's point of view, even if he disagreed with it. He would, most likely, have some emotional sense of what Jordan is experiencing. Charlie evidenced none of this. He judged Jordan to be an "idiot" and simply wrote him off. Like "counter charm,"[1] this is counter communication.

Listening and being able to convey to your partner that he's being listened to is one of the most important aspects of communication. Listening is the manner in which information is conveyed. It's the

---

[1]From a line in the movie "The Boys in the Band," written by Mart Crowley and directed by William Friedkin. 1970. *Source:* www.IMDd.com.

Man Talk: The Gay Couple's Communication Guide
© 2007 by The Haworth Press, Inc. All rights reserved.
doi:10.1300/5527_08

basis for a rational conversation. It's requisite for understanding. It signifies respect and caring and is essential to intimacy. Without listening, there's no communication and there's no relationship.

Cultural Blocks

American culture does not support listening. Listening means you give someone the time to explain himself. It means you cease, at least for the moment, to meet your own needs, and are wholly receptive to what the other person requires. It means you refrain from judging immediately, competing, strategizing, debating, and attacking.

This is not typical of twenty-first century America. As a time-management focused society, we don't have the time to listen to anyone! We want to move along, get to the point, get it over with, and move on. Our obsession with time is not our only problem. We're focused on competing, winning, prevailing, being right, and seeing and hearing only what we want to see and hear. Living this way makes it very difficult to listen to anyone.

What Is Listening?

Listening is an active, rich process, although it may not appear that way. *Hearing* words without thought or interest is undemanding. Looking at someone as he talks but being tuned out takes about as much effort as sleeping. But real listening is work and it involves a number of important elements.

Time Allotment

As I've just mentioned, having the time is a component of listening. You can't rush someone's speech or put an arbitrary deadline on when he has to finish. You also need your own time to understand what he's trying to communicate.

> My mind is thinking *okay, well,* Will & Grace *is coming on in thirty minutes and hopefully this is not going to take longer than thirty minutes.*
>
> Javon, 35, writer
> New Orleans, Louisiana

Concentration

Listening means you have to focus on him and get yourself out of the picture. If he tells you how terribly embarrassed he was, you have to stay away from thinking about the last time you were humiliated. You may think that sharing such an incident is a way to demonstrate identification, and to illustrate that you understand him by telling him that you've been though the same thing. Good listening will communicate insight. Sharing your experience may just be a sneaky way (without you being aware) of talking about yourself. Listening is about him, not you.

Listening requires that the numerous thoughts that soar through your head at any given moment need to be put aside. To know what he's experiencing means your attention has to be undivided. That is not easy to do generally. It's especially difficult if what he says is not particularly interesting or if you find it objectionable.

> . . . it's about really being there . . . allowing yourself to become invested in what you're hearing . . . and not taking anything personally, not in your head determining the value of what's being said, but really just hear what he's saying. And give him an opportunity to express himself and to bitch and to moan and to say whatever he wants . . .
>
> Danny, 31, teacher
> Austin, Texas

> It's about me being there fully for the other person, listening fully to the other person, not being distracted in any other way.
>
> Javon, 35, writer
> New Orleans, Louisiana

If you're in adversarial position with him, it's tempting to plan and strategize your rebuttal as he speaks. This is common. You may also focus on his factual errors and especially note them so as to use as ammunition when you get your turn. This must be avoided because it's the antithesis of communication. Easier said then done, however. In this chapter we explore some techniques to help you with this.

More Than Words

Listening involves attending to nonverbal communication. This encompasses body posture, facial expressions, volume, speed, and tone of voice, eye contact, movement of hands, distance he places between you and him, and congruence, or the lack thereof, between his words and facial expressions. If he tells you that his problem with his boss is minor but his face appears sad and frightened, this is important information to note. If he says he wants to feel more relaxed and open with you but his arms are folded in front of his chest, this is equally significant data.

Giving Up Mind Reading

Although active listening will give you a good idea about what he's experiencing, you don't have the power to read his mind. Telling him what he's thinking is the way to stop communication dead. Even if you're on to something, he may not have any awareness of it. It will therefore have no significance even if you're right. This doesn't mean you can't ask questions and offer a hypothesis if invited to do so. But that's very different from telling him what he's thinking.

In the previous example, where his arms were closed, it would make sense to comment on that. You could say, "I hear you saying that you want to be more open with me, but I see that your arms are folded in front of you as if you want to remain protected. Do you notice that? What do you think of it?" Those are gentle questions that demonstrate your observations and invite your lover to comment. That is very different from saying, "Jeff, you're telling me you want to get close to me but your arms are folded in front of you, which shows that you really don't mean that." That's mind reading.

Asking Questions

Asking questions is appropriate to get a better understanding of what he's saying. He may not have high-quality communicative skills, or if he's upset, it may be particularly difficult for him to explain himself. Gentle questioning, without hidden agendas or implied judgment, can clarify his messages as it tells him you're interested in understanding him. But the timing of asking questions, indeed of speaking at all, is vital.

Do Not Preach

Let's listen to the following conversation between Toby and Rex:

TOBY: She went off on me today, telling me my work was not up to par, that my learning curve was flat. I feel so low, so little. I feel that I'm not a professional, that I can't. . . .

REX: Oh for Christ sakes, it's just a stupid job. Why are you getting so upset? It means nothing. You shouldn't listen to her.

TOBY: Yeah, but I really value my ability to sell. I've always had a good way with people and my sales have always been very high. To tell me that I'm not up to par, that I can't do as well as the other folks . . .

REX: You are making a big deal out of nothing. So it's one job that's not working out. You've only been there a few months. You need to get out of there. Start looking for a new job.

TOBY: I don't want to start that whole process again. I don't want to think that I can't make it there.

REX: You have to get a new job. That's it. Your boss is a bitch and you don't need this.

TOBY: I don't know, Rex . . . I feel so bad.

REX: That's ridiculous; it's only a job, a stupid job.

TOBY: You don't understand . . .

REX: Yes, I do. Start looking for a new job. You have to get out of there.

Rex does mean well. His boyfriend is having a horrible experience on his new job and he wants that to stop. But he's not listening to Toby. Toby is struggling with an assault to his ego. That is the primary issue. Furthermore, he does not, at least at this point, want to look for another job. Rex is not able to appreciate that either. Rex is preaching, and although he wants the best for Toby, he's not helping him achieve that.

> . . . then come the words of wisdom and of commands . . . I shut down . . . I don't like it when he tells me what to do . . . it's about my independence; it hurts my independence . . .
>
> Aidan, 37, physical therapist
> Tampa, Florida

Don't Rush to Judgment (and Be Gentle When You Do)

People are not value neutral, and we are forever making judgments about ourselves and others. If your boyfriend tells you that he plans to buy a new car on credit cards, and you know that he's unemployed and doesn't have savings, you're going to judge this to be a gravely unwise decision. Judging is part of human interaction; it's how you express your view and the timing of that expression that matters.

Listening requires that you have the whole story before you voice your appraisal. Perhaps he will start off saying this only to let you know that he would love to buy a car, but really has no intention to do so. Or maybe this is his way of telling you that his reality is so awful that he doesn't want to face it anymore. If you listen to the whole story, you may find that he eventually tells you he's very depressed and the car issue vanishes. If you judge precipitously, you could stop the full narrative from unfolding.

Judgment also has a negative connotation. This derives from judging with malice, which involves, among other negative attributes, attack and usually attack of the whole person. Telling your boyfriend he's stupid, bad, horrible, terrible, pathetic, etc., is that kind of judging. It need not be that way.

Let's look at this example. If in fact your boyfriend is planning to buy a car under these circumstances, you don't have to say "you're nuts." You could address his frustration and gently point out how destructive buying a new car at such a time could be. It could go something like this:

> *Leo, I realize how miserable it must feel to have no savings and no job. But if you buy a new car on credit cards, you're going to put yourself in a much worse position. You know the kind of interest they charge; you could get yourself in real big trouble. How are you going to pay the interest, let alone the principal? Why not wait at least until you get employed again?*

Of course, he still may not listen to you. He doesn't have to. Judging is not the same thing as commanding or controlling. If he doesn't agree with your stance, there's really nothing you can do. He forever remains a free agent. When we resort to insults and threats in order to influence the outcome ("you're irresponsible if you buy a car and I'm going to let everyone know what an asshole you are") that's when it becomes toxic. I recognize that having a boyfriend who exercises poor judgment is not easy to live with, and you may decide that you can't live with him. That is very different, however, from attempting to *make* him refrain from doing what you consider inappropriate.

Silence Is Wonderful

Silence can be wonderful. Sometimes the best, but most difficult thing to do is to say nothing. A very crucial part of listening is to let your partner speak without interruption. This is a judgment call, when to remain silent and when to comment or ask questions. One indication that points to the former is when your partner is describing an extremely upsetting event or issue. You could ask as he begins to tell his story if he would like you to remain silent until he finishes. Or you could simply wait until he gives you a cue. He may say at one point "what do you think?" and that would be your invitation. Absent of that, just remain silent and listen. Of course you will respond with "uh huh," "yes," and "I see" to demonstrate that you're paying attention. Good eye contact on your part is also essential. Giving your advice or trying to reassure precipitously can be interpreted by him as insensitivity and cut off his surge of emotion.

You may question how saying something can be so off the mark. Premature advice or reassurance is of no value emotionally because one first needs to go through the process of *telling*. If he just informed you that he's been fired, for example, he needs to articulate his thoughts and feelings, to discharge his fear and anger, and to make sense of what is an ego deflating, life-changing event. If you tell him that he's going to be okay, that you'll take care of the bills, that he needs to do this or that, you're not letting him go through what he needs to go through at that moment.

He needs the undivided floor because it allows his pain to find full expression. Your silence gives him center stage, which underscores the meaningfulness of his experience. Your silence conveys you're a witness to his predicament; he's not going through this alone. This is powerful support. Trying to take away his pain at this juncture, as noble a goal as that is, will not achieve that. You cut off the process of him telling his story. He may thank you for your good intentions but recognize on some level that something doesn't feel right. That's because he wasn't heard.

The Difficulty with Silence

Many of us have difficulty with being silent, especially when someone is relating a heartbreaking or otherwise difficult experience.

Living in a culture that prizes "doing" and "producing" and "assertiveness," silence feels like the antithesis to this. It feels like you're doing nothing.

Silence can also be anxiety provoking for the listener. If your lover is relating a story, and then pauses for a while (and this is particularly likely when someone is upset and confused) it can feel uncomfortable as you both sit there with nothing being said. It is awkward for you. Awkwardness creates anxiety, and that anxiety may then propel you to say something just to break that pause. But he likely needs the pause to reflect and continue when he's ready. By saying something, you interfere with his need as you satisfy *yours*.

I don't mean to imply that this is a selfish act on your part. You may not be aware of this dynamic, and it's reasonable, certainly, to want to avoid feeling awkward. By being alert to this you can avoid what's intuitive, but which compromises listening. Sitting through the silence means you're following his beat. Your support for him will shine as your intimacy grows.

The Danger of His Emotional World

When you truly listen to another person, you enter, on an emotional level, his world. If he's depressed and miserable and frightened, to some degree you experience those emotions. This is one of the occupational hazards of being a therapist. To help someone you have to visit his world and feel his experience from the inside. Yet you must maintain your boundaries and not live his experience. This can be challenging and uncomfortable; it takes awareness and work.

This process exists in any kind of true listening, and is far more challenging for you and your lover because you're emotionally involved with each other. Therapists are not emotionally involved to the same degree with their clients, and are trained to maintain boundaries. If it's difficult for us, it's far more challenging when it's the man you love. But if you really want to know him, you have to take this risk.

For example, if your boyfriend's mother is dying, and he talks about his profound sadness, it will be disturbing to witness his pain. That's when you may change the subject or suddenly realize that you have to be somewhere else. I suggest you stay with him and your feelings. It will hurt, but you get to *know* him, and that's a privilege.

Discomfort is just discomfort, not decimation. Make peace with discomfort and you'll enhance intimacy.

The Shock of Knowing Yourself

Listening means learning about yourself in a way that you never have. The serious men in your life get to know you, sometimes better than you know yourself. Self-awareness has its limitations. You're inside yourself, in a manner of speaking, and therefore it's difficult to always accurately appreciate how you appear on the outside. When you have an audience of one who's there most of the time, he has knowledge you can't have. On occasion, it's not knowledge you necessarily want to acquire!

As imperfect creatures, we have our petty, annoying, irrational, pain-in-the-ass attributes. Our partners know this, in fact suffer through them, and want to share that experience with the objects of their torment, namely us! Of course, if you are attacked it's very difficult to listen. Attack creates defense, and that ends listening. But some men consider any criticism an attack, and if that's you, it's imperative to re-evaluate how you deal with criticism.

Listening about how you negatively impact your partner gives you an opportunity to improve your relationship and grow as an individual. The aim should not be perfection, and his criticism should be something you do or don't do, *not who you are.*

It's never easy to listen to disapproval, especially about something you're not aware of. If you have problems with self-esteem, it will be that more difficult because it will feed into the global negative feelings you have about yourself. Your instinctive response will be to discredit what he's saying and stop listening.

I would make a Herculean effort to avoid that. One way to achieve this is to remind yourself that imperfections never make you a horrible human being, and that all of us have our share of flaws. Furthermore, you don't have to agree with him, and he certainly could be mistaken. By listening you acquire an opportunity to assess and negotiate. You foreclose that if you don't. A number of exercises can help sharpen your listening skills.

Acquiring Information

As I mentioned earlier, concentration is paramount yet it can be difficult, particularly with emotionally charged issues. You can sharpen this skill by practicing listening when the issue is not intense.

This first exercise can help you focus on facts. Try this out with a friend. I'm suggesting not trying this with your partner because it's important to minimize the possibility of emotions entering the picture. This is an exercise in *fact* detection. Obviously, in the real world, fact and emotion intertwine. Learning, however, works best in steps. If there's tension between the two of you, even the most benign subject could get charged.

Have your friend tell you a story for about ten minutes. He can tell you about something that happened at work, a trip he took recently, or anything that involves a number of facts. He should know the details of the story well, such as time sequences, the different characters involved, who said what, the setting, etc. After he finishes, let him quiz you about it, asking you for at least five important elements of the story. Since you're motivated to listen because you'll be quizzed, this should help you focus on the data (no taking notes). Become aware of thoughts that have nothing to do with what he's talking about (what you're having for dinner, etc.), memories of how something like this happened to you long ago, etc. As those distractions appear, immediately focus your attention back on your friend, and try to get rid of the distractions. Visualize a picture of a stop sign and internally yell, "Stop," "shut up," or "go away." Use only a microsecond for that and then focus right back on your friend. Each time a distraction appears, repeat the process.

You'll learn how to focus and will also discover how much information you're taking in or missing. Repeat this exercise as often as you need to. The goal is to be able to clearly remember those five facts (you could try more if you'd like), understand them (not just be able repeat what you heard), and communicate that understanding to your friend.

Learning to Observe Body Language

Listening involves appreciating and attending to the rich source of information in body language. How we stand, move, where our eyes go, the way the muscles in our faces change to create expressions, the distance we place between ourselves and others, our posture, etc., communicate powerful messages. Any movie actor knows the importance of this. Film is primarily a visual medium, and body communication is key to portraying the story. The next time you watch a movie, take note of how much you learn without anything being said.

An exercise you can use to enhance your attentiveness to and comprehension of body communication is to watch TV with the sound turned off. I suggest watching "talking heads" news shows to get a good sense how faces change during different emotions. Record the show so you can go back and hear later on what was said. Watch, also, some physical action DVD movies with the volume turned off. Observe different kinds of messages communicated with the full body. As with the talking head shows, go back later on to hear what was said. Obviously, you need not watch an entire show this way, only some segments. Use your judgment.

As you watch with the volume turned off, make note of what you see and what that means. For example, tight eyes may mean anger to you. Getting physically close may communicate readiness to fight or intimacy, depending on other body language (such as smiling versus scowling). Write out on a piece of paper the physical expression and then next to that what you believe is being communicated. Use two vertical columns. Later on, go back to the segment, turn on the volume, and see if what is being said correlates with what you determined to be communicated via body language. Keep in mind that the two will not always correlate, but that doesn't mean that you're incorrect. Politicians, for example, are famous for calling their political nemesis (and sometimes real life enemies) "my good friend" with a smile that could kill. Just think of President Bush's smile. (I'm sorry—I just had to throw that in!) This exercise will prime your skill to read nonverbal communication.

Listening When You Disagree

Listening when you disagree is very difficult for many people because disagreements tend to ignite emotions, and emotions can obliterate rationality. Exploring the following exercises will help you with this.

As with the first exercise, I want you to call on a friend again. Have a dialogue with her about something you disagree with. It should not, however, involve a major conflict. It can be complex, however, like divergent political views, or simple, like whether a movie is good or bad. You could revisit an old disagreement or have one that comes spontaneously in the course of a conversation.

As she speaks, ask yourself what she needs, what's she seeing, what's her frame of reference that brings her to the conclusions she has. Picture yourself in her place, and try to imagine that you could see it the same way if you were her. Entertain the possibility that your position is not the whole story.

Observe your reactions. You are likely to have thoughts that tell you why she's "wrong" and you're "right." You're apt to have musings that focus on the fallacy and weak points of her position. You may also be contemplating how her actions will negatively affect you. For example, your disagreement may be over wanting to go to dinner alone with her while she'd rather hang out with you and her boyfriend in a bar. And you don't like her boyfriend and hate bars!

Work hard to dispel those thoughts and considerations (utilize the technique described above to avoid distracting thoughts) as you focus on understanding her point of reference. Let go of the wish "to be right" and to "win." Put your interests aside for the moment. *Make it your only goal to fully understand where she's coming from.*

Learning from Television

Your television is a gold mine of opportunities to practice listening to what you oppose. Any show that has people discussing their views is fertile ground. CNN, MSNBC, and the Fox News Network are excellent sources of these kinds of broadcasts. The Sunday morning news shows such as *Face the Nation* on NBC also provide outstanding opportunities to learn how to listen.

You can practice the same exercise I just described by listening to someone whose point you don't share. I suggest trying this with a figure with whom you have extremely divergent views, such as a politician you can't stand.

Simply watch the interview and practice the same mental exercises I've suggested you do with your friend. As absurd and contemptible as his position may be, stay completely away from judging and focus on understanding his frame of reference. Keep in mind that understanding is not agreeing. The more outrageous his views, the more of a challenge certainly, but the better you can sharpen your listening skills. The biggest idiot can be your best teacher!

Writing It Out

Choose someone you're in conflict with (or have been in conflict with where the problem was *not* resolved) and write a few lines or paragraphs arguing his point of view. You won't know what he's actually thinking or thought and that's okay. You're not attempting to mind read. You're trying to construct on paper how he may view the issue you disagree over. Write it out as if you were him. This will make it easier to appreciate his view because you will "become him" for the moment. This exercise may be difficult, especially if you're convinced of your position and are angry with this person. Again, the bigger the challenge, the more you can learn how to listen.

Let's look at the following situation as an example. A good friend repeatedly declines invitations from you to get together. You're aware he's busy but you miss your time with him and feel ignored. You're angry and hurt and feel that if he were really a good friend, he would find a way to find the time.

You could write something like this (remember you're now him):

> I guess Johnny *(that's you)* must be unhappy with me. But this project at work is killing me. It can break me if I don't come through by deadline. I only have a month for this, which is crazy, but there can be no extension. The fall items have to be shipped. Next week I'll be working late every night and I'm going have to go in at least part of the day on Saturday and Sunday. Goddamn it, I'm exhausted. I'd love to get together with Johnny, but where am I going to find the time now? If he's a real friend, he should understand. This is our biggest client and I'll be toast if I screw this up. This is my priority because I have to eat. I can't stretch myself any further.

This is not a direct listening exercise, but it affords you practice in giving serious consideration to another person's view when you disagree. That's a key component of being able to listen under those circumstances.

Cultural Challenges

As we've seen, listening is a complicated and demanding business. It becomes even more so when you and your partner don't share the same rules of the road.

That can happen if you're in an intercultural relationship. Some cultures have vastly different rules about communication, and you may find yourself violating rules without ever knowing they existed. When I was in Greece, long ago, I noticed a group of young men openly holding hands. I thought I had found "family," but I had not. Their behavior had nothing to do with being gay. (No, I didn't go over to them and make a fool of myself. I figured it out!)

Intercultural relationships create special challenges. Words, gestures, even the appropriateness of discussing problems can vary widely. This is certainly surmountable, but that's predicated on having a least some knowledge of the forces creating those challenges. We'll explore this in the next chapter.

Chapter 8

Cultural Exchange: Communicating in Interracial Relationships

(Jack is a thirty-five-year-old Jewish man who was born and has lived all of his life in New York City. Joey is a twenty-seven-year-old Filipino man who moved to New York five years ago. He has been with Jack for nine months. Jack had just come home from work. Joey had arrived a few minutes earlier with take-out food. He had the key to Jack's apartment. It was a Tuesday evening.)

JACK: [loudly and excited] Hey Joey, I'm taking off Friday. Let's go upstate for the weekend. Hell, you don't work on Friday so it should work. I know a great B&B. You'll love it.

JOEY: That does sound great. But what's a B&B?

JACK: A bed-and-breakfast, silly. What, are you stupid?

JOEY: That was rude.

JACK: What was rude?

JOEY: Calling me stupid.

JACK: [walking closer to Joey] Oh, I'm only kidding, you idiot! Come on, this is going to be great! A hot bed-and-breakfast in the middle of the woods! What could be better? So I'll call the place?

JOEY: [silence]

JACK: [walking even closer] I'm going to call, okay?

JOEY: [silence]

JACK: What's wrong?

JOEY: [stepping back from Jack] Why are you yelling at me?

JACK: I'm not yelling [louder]. I'm happy. I haven't had an extra day off in months. I can't wait to do this. Come on, it'll be great.

JOEY: You're scaring me. You seem so wild.

JACK: Scaring you? What the hell are you talking about?

JOEY: I'm not going anywhere with you.

JACK: What?

JOEY: [silence]

JOEY: I'm not going.

JACK: What's with you? You love stuff like this. Why don't you want to go?

JOEY: Because you're screaming at me, and you're scaring me, and you're insulting me, and you look like you've gone crazy.

JACK: Are you out of your fucking mind? I'm not screaming; I'm happy, goddamn it!

JOEY: You're crazy.

JACK: You're a miserable killjoy.

JOEY: [silence]

JACK: Fuck you. I'll go without you.

JOEY: I'm leaving.

Not the way to plan a relaxing, mini vacation in the forest!

Jack was excited and happy and suggesting an activity that both of them could enjoy. Joey was also interested in it. There was no disagreement or unresolved animosity between them. Yet it turned into a disaster. What happened?

The devil was in the divergent communication rules each of these men lived by. In Jack's world getting excited and raising the volume of his voice when happy was normal. So was moving closer to someone he was sharing his joy with. Saying words like "stupid" and "idiot" was a form of joking that had no mal intent. Joey's world couldn't be more different. Jack's loud voice and movement toward him appeared to be out of control, threatening behavior. The words "idiot" and "stupid" were insults to his intelligence. Neither Jack nor Joey understood each other's communication rules, and therefore couldn't understand each other.

Culture, Race, and Communication

Culture and *race* are powerfully loaded words in American society, describing complex matters that have dissimilar meanings for different people. For the purpose of examining their impact on couple communication, I'm going to define these words in very limited, simplistic terms. I refer to race as the ethnic group you identify yourself with, and culture as the set of life rules you internalize *as a result* of being in a particular group. Keep in mind that your racial group may have only a partial and less important impact on your culture than other group factors. For example, a middle-class African-American person living in suburban Connecticut, and a poor African-American individual living in South Central Los Angeles, are impacted more by their respective economic groups than by the color of their skin.

We are all part of multiple cultures. A gay Catholic Mexican American is impacted by American and Mexican culture, the culture of his religion, and the culture of being gay.

Different cultures create different rules about communication. I'm not referring to language barriers which, when present, add additional challenges. Many aspects of communication vary depending on your background. As we witnessed in the example of Jack and Joey, loud and excited speech had very different meanings because of cultural factors.

This chapter is *not* going to be about learning various communication rules in a variety of cultures. Attempting to describe that would require volumes. If you're in an interracial/intercultural relationship, and having trouble getting through to each other, cultural and racial issues may be playing a role. The aim of this chapter is to elucidate that, and describe some of the kinds of problematic areas where this can manifest.

The Danger of Generalizations and Assumptions

Sensitivity to these issues is vastly different from having knee-jerk assumptions about race and culture. Concluding that your lover is behaving a certain way because of his background is as culturally incompetent as having no clue to the possibility of that influence. Sensitivity means that you are aware of a *possibility* and then explore further. In the previous example, it would have been helpful if Jack wondered what "excitement" meant in Filipino culture, and then *asked Joey about it.* For him to assume that Joey will react a certain way because he's Filipino is erroneous and destructive. Another Filipino man may have reacted differently.

This bears repeating, and I apologize if you get it already! We're individuals, not statistics, *and no matter what you know or think you know about a racial group or a culture does not give you specific information about any particular person.* Sensitivity means curiosity, wanting to learn, listening as we've covered in the previous chapter, and asking questions. That is the way you improve your communication and your relationship.

Please also note that I will comment at times about characteristics of specific cultures and their impact on biracial, bicultural relationships. These comments, while derived from fact, *are generalizations and limited in their scope. They make no assumptions about individuals nor are they impervious to alternative interpretations.*

The Life of Your Relationship

The "life" of a relationship comprises the daily interactions that weave together over time to create the pattern of being with someone. For example, you may both work separately during the day and come together in the evening to share a meal, discuss things that happened to each of you, and fall asleep together. On weekends you shop together and share the tasks of cleaning and laundry. When it comes to making important decisions, no choice is made without both of you participating.

With sex, you may have a preference but are willing and desirous of trying something new. Perhaps you view yourself as a bottom, but on occasion want to be a top. He complies.

The life of your relationship depends, among other factors, on a shared set rules and values. When there's no bilateral buy in there will be problems. If you and your lover are from different backgrounds, this could happen.

As Americans males, we have our share of issues. Some cultures, however, have extremely inflexible rules about what males can do. Shopping, doing laundry, and cooking are roles that are reserved exclusively for females. "Equalitarian" is an unfamiliar concept. When it comes to major decisions, the man makes them.

In a study published in *Sex Roles: A Journal of Research* by Marcela Raffaelli she found that socialization of males and females in Latino families in America varied significantly. Adolescent boys were given significantly more freedom (staying out later, having a car, etc.) while females were expected to perform domestic chores.[1]

If your lover refuses to participate in chores, is he being unfair and lazy, or is this a violation of a cultural rule he adheres to? If he thinks he should make the important decisions, is he simply being pig-

---

[1]Raffaelli, Marcela. Gender Socialization in Latino/a families: Results from two retrospective studies. In *Sex Roles: A Journal of Research* March, 2004.

headed, or reacting to a "higher authority?" What about being anally penetrated? Should he refuse to be fucked, is he adverse to trying something new, cares nothing about your feelings, or does this mean the end of his manhood? Could he feel, given his background, that being gay is difficult enough, and getting it up the ass is over the line? These are vastly different reasons. Being a jerk and inflexible is not sympathetic. Having to struggle with internal edicts is.

To find out, you have to be alert to the possibility of cultural factors. You lover also has to be alert to your cultural expectations and not categorically conclude that you're spoiled and demanding. Both of you must talk and listen. You may ask, "Is there something about your family background that makes cooking and laundry a problem for you? Do the men in your culture make all the decisions and is it confusing for you to be with another man?" He may ask: "Why must you have a say in all the decisions? Why is my doing the dishes so important to you? Do you feel that I'm not treating you right?"

This kind of a conversation gives both of you information. Important information. Being blind to cultural influences forecloses that. "Blindness" can cause you to live in two angry, separate worlds where neither of you know what is really going on.

Of course cultural sensitivity doesn't solve the problem in itself, but it's an opening. It gives you the opportunity to find dialogue to understand one another. Sometimes understanding is enough and you can live with limitations because of the other value you derive from the relationship. Sometimes it's a catalyst for change.

The Closet

At this time in gay American history, the closet is a hot political issue. Many feel that it's unconscionable to hide, especially at this time of massive social change. Aim has been taken at those with power and prestige to come out either voluntarily or be forced out. Thus, the concept of outing.

Being in a relationship where each of you have different attitudes about being open about your sexual orientation is a significant challenge. How you relate to your jobs, families, or even walking down the street can become issues of contention.

Many factors affect comfort with being open. One issue is culture. Cultural imperatives in some groups consider homosexuality deeply shameful, and being gay as bestowing shame upon the family. This exists in some Asian cultures and causes a sort of double whammy because there's a strong focus on family ties. To be close to your family and live an openly gay lifestyle can be momentously problematic.

If you're in a relationship (in this example I'm assuming "you" are Caucasian American and "he" is an Asian American), and you're out and he's not, you're in an uncomfortable situation. Your life with him is, in many ways, compromised. You may want to confront him for his lack of courage and his shame for not being himself. Unfortunately, there's plenty of political permission these days to do just that. I wouldn't be confrontational, however.

Coming out of the closet is a developmental process, not a moral test. It involves feeling progressively more comfortable with one's sexual orientation and going through an identity transformation. Badgering your lover about his "lack of courage and guts" is moralization of a complex process. Cultural rules of the ones I've just described add exponentially to his challenge. Your task is to be sensitive to this (despite your righteous frustration). It's your lover's responsibility to be receptive to your feelings.

I would open a dialogue about what being out means to him and his family. Try to understand what his sense of "shame" means to him and bringing that upon his family. You're likely to see it as a very powerful and difficult conflict for him. For his part, he needs to appreciate how this inhibits you in your love for him. His being in the closet, and being in a relationship with you, makes the issue your problem, not just his. It's important for him to appreciate that.

You're not likely to resolve this in one or even multiple conversations. Having the dialogue, nevertheless, enables each of you to appreciate each other's challenge. Hopefully his understanding of your feelings and his commitment to his life with you will help him experiment with small steps of change. This can't be "hurried up" despite both of your desiring to do so.

Family Ties

Many factors affect how close and involved you are as an adult with your family of origin. As American society has become increasingly mobile, it's not unusual for many of us to live thousands of miles from our parents and siblings. Our connections are thus weakened by geography. If there are strong cultural expectations to remain close, however, those ties will remain strong despite distance. In some instances the in-laws will live around the corner just for that reason.

Strong family ties can be wonderful or not so wonderful depending on your point of view. Perhaps you have few family relationships and your boyfriend's family becomes a kind of surrogate for you. You may become best friends with his mother! On the other hand, you may not want them in your life, or at least in small doses. When you marry your boyfriend, you're not marrying his mother or other members of his family. In cultures with strong family relationships, however, you do get two (or more) for the price of one! Don't underestimate the power of their influence, from their approval (or the lack thereof) of you, to the amount of time he spends with them, and to important decisions he makes.

For example, in Filipino culture, close family ties are expected. While it falls far more on the adult female to take care of the parents, boys are also expected to remain loyal and involved with the family.

Strong family connections impact relationships. Family members don't have to be in your presence to affect you. For example, your lover may feel the need to visit them often, which means he has less time for just the two of you. If he's in the closet and you *can't* show up on family occasions, you're not going to be happy. His family may not even know of your existence. If you're out and integrate your sexual orientation into most of your life, this will feel strange and very uncomfortable.

There are other potential consequences. You may want to go on a trip to Rome but he has to visit his grandmother's grave because it would have been her one-hundredth birthday. You may think his choice is absurd; he may think you're absurd for questioning him. His family may throw guilt trips on him when he does something they don't endorse. It may be easy for you to say he has to grow up and "leave home," but not as easy for him to do it.

There can be a blurry line between cultural expectations and enmeshment, where your lover is essentially living his life for his family. You must be careful, however about pathologizing and advising. Nothing says louder "I don't understand you" than declaring that his cultural norms are abnormal. On the other hand, if he's telling you that he's frustrated and guilty and depressed because he's not meeting his family expectations, that's an inroad to a conversation Be gentle and inquisitive; do not jump to conclusions or recommendations. Those ties are still very strong and the wrong approach will backfire. You'll find him defending his family to you.

No matter what his cultural expectations are, you still matter. He's an adult and he's *made a choice* to be in an adult relationship with you. If his bond with his family is causing serious problems for you, it's imperative that you express this. Cultural understanding works both ways; it's a matter of appreciating where each of you are coming from, having respect for the importance of your relationship, and trying to strike a balance between your differing cultural beliefs.

Cultural Beliefs About Open Discussion

In some groups, the open expression of issues is not considered appropriate. In particular, adversarial kinds of communication are to be avoided and one is supposed to "read between the lines" and "take a hint." Saying "no," for example, is considered rude and hurts someone's feelings. Yet the person still means no; you're just supposed to have figured it out. You may have asked for a favor, for instance. He doesn't say no, maybe even says yes, but when it comes to complying with the request, he doesn't.

For someone not raised in this kind of culture, such a rule will seem maddening. You're likely to conclude that the person is simply a liar and a flake and maybe even crazy.

If this is your lover, you have a formidable problem on your hands. Since open discussion is not part of his cultural repertoire, it will be difficult to even address the rule.

Throughout this book, I have maintained that clear, direct, open communication is imperative in any relationship. As I've indicated, not all cultures share this perspective. I nevertheless maintain that it's mandatory for your relationship to be viable.

The best course of action you can take in a situation like this is to be aware that this may be operating, and then try, in a gentle way, to approach him. The power of your bond may enable him to share with you what's going on, and to even modify his behavior. I would expect that even in the most optimistic situations, however, this would be neither easy nor immediate.

If you were raised in such a culture, I agree that making a change is a massive adjustment to something that will feel foreign and wrong. You may not want to change or even be capable of changing. You certainly have a right to maintain what feels appropriate for you. I also own that my view is a value I hold, not a universal law of nature like gravity. Nevertheless, in my professional work with gay men, and as a gay man in a long-term relationship, I see no possibility of growth and happiness and viability unless there is open, clear, and direct communication.

That Dirty Word Called Racism

> . . . when (we) go into a . . . store . . . (I'm) be watched and observed, and he's being helped . . . that's a big difference.
>
> Javon, 35, writer
> New Orleans, Louisiana,
> who is African American and is referring
> to himself and his white boyfriend

You may have thought that by the dawn of the twenty-first century we would have risen above this. Perhaps a hundred years hence racism will exist only as a peculiar concept in history books. In the present, unfortunately, racism is alive and well and is as virulent as ever.

If you are white in American society, you are afforded a privilege you may not even be aware of: the freedom to be left alone. Many people of color don't enjoy that. Whether it's being stopped by the police for being in the "wrong" neighborhood, paid unwarranted attention in a store, or avoided on the street, white folks simply don't have to put up with this. Of course this is only one of many privileges that some assume and others are denied. This creates two very different realities in bi-racial/bi-cultural relationships.

Certainly there have been massive changes. Early twenty-first century is not mid-twentieth century. That's good, but the poison of racism is deeply embedded in the sole of society, and the work of eradicating its existence hasn't even begun.

> (he asked me) "Are you active in politics?" . . . I wanted to say to him, "Well, I'm black, and I'm a gay male . . . every breath I take is political."
>
> Javon, 35, writer
> New Orleans, Louisiana

As a person who does not experience this kind of discrimination but is in love with someone who does, you are likely to be concerned and outraged. That's also good, but it's not the same as living day by day, hour by hour, as your boyfriend does.

You may declare that you know what it's like because you're gay in a homophobic society. There is one crucial difference. Despite stereotypes, most of us gay folks are thoroughly invisible to our enemies. That is not an option when your skin or eyes or other physical attributes aren't white.

What are the implications for your relationship? If you're white, it is acknowledging that there's much you don't know, being open to learning, and expanding your zone of sensitivity. When your lover tells you that he doesn't feel comfortable in a certain neighborhood or certain part of the country, find out what's going on. Listen. Don't assume he's overreacting. When he sees the look of a suspicion in the eyes of a store clerk that you didn't see, don't assume your vision is better. It just may be the opposite. Those victimized by racism can literally see what someone who is not persecuted cannot see.

If you're a person of color with a white lover you need to accept that he has and will always have a different reality. Nevertheless, you can teach him about yours. If he can hear you and be *respectful* of your view, that's a lot. His response can translate into a qualitative difference in your relationship. Perhaps he has no problem with all-white vacation resorts. However, if he can understand that it's not okay for you, and be willing to change vacations plans, that counts for a lot.

You also need to be sensitive to his view. Perhaps you sense racism when it's not actually there. Maybe you thought a friend of his had an attitude toward you because you're black, when he did not. Having sensitivity to racism can sometimes put your antennas into overdrive. You may have better "eyes" but he may know his friend better. Perhaps his friend doesn't like anyone, white, green or blue! His attitude has nothing to do with your race. Listen, avoid jumping to conclusions, and respect his perspective. That's the essence of communication.

Internalized Racism

Now we are going to visit a place you may not want to go to: the issue of widespread internalized racism; racism within ourselves.

Racism is rightfully shunned as a destructive, evil force proliferated by ignorance, hate, and small-mindedness. Overt expression of racist thinking is one of the most unaccepted viewpoints in mainstream American society. We don't hear much of it nowadays, and when it happens, there's appropriate condemnation and serious consequences. Certainly massive positive change has occurred in society, particularly in the past fifty years. That's not the same thing as eradication of racism, or anything remotely close to it.

As with homophobia, when we are exposed to thousands, perhaps millions of racist messages throughout life, it's impossible to remove that from our collective psyche. We are sensitive to racial differences in people, and unfortunately, make judgments based solely on those differences. Sometimes the judgments are even positive and subtle but to the object of those judgments they are no less hurtful and obnoxious.

Many years ago I had an African-American lover. He was almost six feet tall, lean, and athletic looking. He did not know anything about basketball, did not ever play basketball, and probably would have been bad at it. Yet when we went to a party strangers would approach him by saying "I bet you play basketball." It irked him to no end and he immediately informed the person that he knew nothing about basketball. These people didn't mean harm but their assumption that he played basketball because he was black and tall is a supposition based on the racist assumption that "all young, tall black men play basketball." Sounds harmless, huh? Maybe not. How distant is that from the supposition that "all young black men in white neighborhoods at night are up to no good?" Not far, because the dynamics are the same: basing decisions on skin color, not individuals. That is racist thinking.

Are the vast majority of us committing harmful racist acts toward others? Of course not. Would most of us be appalled if we did something unintentional that produced hurt in another innocent human being? Certainly. Reasonable, rational folks shudder at the thought of racism. So why is it important we acknowledge that we harbor some of these of kind of thoughts? *Because they are there whether we want them or not,* and acknowledgment eliminates denial, develops sensitivity, and imparts truth. That is always good for a relationship. If you are walking around believing that there isn't a racist microthought in your body, you're being dishonest with yourself and others. If your lover is of color and faces institutional racism on a daily basis, he's going to know how foolhardy that position is. It can create problems with him because it says that you are clueless to a very important part of his daily life experience. It can stifle communication when, for example, your Mexican-American attorney lover tells you he was mistaken for the cleaning person at his office, and you don't see why he has a problem with it.

Awareness in ourselves produces sensitivity to the issue in general and helps produce affirmative change.

You're likely to think twice before assuming that a black man in "your white neighborhood" doesn't belong there, or a Latino man is not adequately qualified for a job you can offer. That is palpable change, good for yourself, your relationship, and society.

Bridges That Can't Be Built

Intercultural/interracial relationships, as all relationships, create challenges. It's not easy to find the place where two separate human beings experience profound connection and contentment. Love requires bridge building, and that can't always be achieved. Sometimes bridges are built, only to come crashing down years later.

Poor communication can destroy a relationship, but miscommunication can also be symptomatic of relationship meltdown. The yelling, accusations, and high drama occur because the couple's fundamental bond is unraveling. There are infinite reasons why people break up. Sometimes it's related to long-standing communication problems and other causes. Occasionally relationships die for no clear-cut rationale; people change and what they needed at one time they no longer need nor want.

Relationships in serious trouble do not necessarily mean dissolution, but the risk of that is very high. This is a terrifying reality, especially for men who have been together a long time.

Poor communication can signify that the problems are so deep and wide that it's impossible to get through to each other without a fundamental change in the underlying problems. For example, anger can be so intense that neither man wants to or even has the capacity to listen any longer. This is the time for professional intervention. Other times the die is already cast and poor communication is also the way some folks dance around this fact. As long as there's noise, as long as there's high drama and accusations and plentiful blame, no one has to face the truth that it's over. In a situation like this, improving communication, if possible and with professional intervention, will help the couple separate, not improve on a foundation that has been obliterated.

In the next chapter we look at these kinds of relationships, as well as distinguish them from couples that still have a fighting chance.

Chapter 9

Communication Problems As a Warning Sign: Coming to Terms with Relationship Meltdown

ARTHUR: Why do you have to go out with Tim and Cameron again without me?

TITO: Look, these are my friends—I like to spend time with them without you. We don't have to do everything together. What's wrong with that?

ARTHUR: I feel left out. You spend more time with them than you do with me.

TITO: That's not true.

ARTHUR: It is.

TITO: Well, maybe if you weren't so miserable all the time and screwed up all my fun I'd want to be with you.

ARTHUR: What? Since when is this?

TITO: Like you didn't know, you scumbag.

ARTHUR: No, I don't know what you're talking about.

TITO: I'm going out. See you later.

ARTHUR: Don't go anywhere. You're throwing bullshit at me again. Who are you fucking now?

TITO: After that little fuck fest with your co-worker Mickey . . . that I only found out because of Rachael. I think you got some nerve.

ARTHUR: I don't have anything to say about that.

TITO: Fine. I'm out of here. See you later.

ARTHUR: You need to talk to me about spending all of this time out of the house.

TITO. I'm not talking to you.

ARTHUR: You're selfish and mean. You're such an uncaring fuck.

TITO: You should talk. It's always about you. Everything is always about you. Fuck you.

ARTHUR: Fuck you too.

TITO: God give me some peace from this motherfucker.

Man Talk: The Gay Couple's Communication Guide
© 2007 by The Haworth Press, Inc. All rights reserved.
doi:10.1300/5527_10

ARTHUR: You started all of this tonight. Everything would be fine if you cared a little more about our relationship. You create all the problems and then blame everything on me.

TITO: Maybe if you weren't such a miserable prick I'd care more.

ARTHUR: Do you know how bad this makes me feel when you talk to me like this?

TITO: I don't care how you feel anymore.

Arthur and Tito had been coming apart for a long time. Years of miscommunication, going in different directions, and deep discontent had finally killed it for both of them.

Tito had changed a great deal in the three years he'd been with Arthur. When they first met, Tito felt very lonely and desperately wanted to be with someone. Being in a relationship, at that time, was his number one goal in life. At thirty-six, he had a very different perspective. Two of his close friends had died during the period of his relationship, one the innocent victim of a robbery, the other from leukemia. Jim was twenty-four when he was shot and Martha was twenty-seven when she died.

Tito realized how valuable time was. He became conscious of how much he wanted to change his career and move to New York City. They lived in Seattle. Arthur would not hear of it.

Tito wanted to explore different kinds of sexual experiences. Arthur only laughed. He had no interest and wasn't willing to disturb his comfort zone. Sex between them became mechanical, stale, and eventually nonexistent. Tito began having affairs and then felt guilty and dirty. He also felt increasing anger toward Arthur. This resulted in attacking Arthur over minor issues. Arthur accurately sensed that Tito was upset with something else. He felt unfairly attacked and repeatedly demanded that Tito tell him what was wrong. Tito had only one answer: "nothing."

Tito began questioning much of life. What was his purpose on earth? What was happiness all about? He became interested in his family roots, returned to the church, and seemed to be continuously filled with questions.

Arthur had no interest in any of this. He felt that Tito's changes were a bunch of nonsense. He was insensitive to Tito's losses and felt it was time he moved on. He concluded that Tito was in an early middle-age crisis. All Arthur wanted, he told himself, was a normal relationship with a normal man. Now he had this! He felt stuck with a whining, complaining, questioning everything individual. Tito disinterested and irritated him. He felt cheated and disappointed and grew to resent him. The resentment was mutual.

Going out with friends was Tito's way of getting relief from a very unhappy home situation. He knew that he no longer wanted to be with Arthur but somehow couldn't bring himself to address this directly. They lived together, and despite all his desires for change and seizing the moment, it was just too scary for him to make such a radical change. Arthur also knew that the relationship had stopped working. He knew he was unhappy, but if Tito would just change, he convinced himself, all would be better!

This conversation we witnessed had nothing to do with getting through to each other any longer. That process, for them, had ended long ago. It was rather a bilateral expression of deep discontent, a way to express the issue of incompatibility without really saying it! It doesn't get more dysfunctional that this. Their poor communication served as a means to avoid acknowledging that their relationship was dead as a doornail and that they needed to separate.

Problematic Relationships That Don't Need to End

Signs of serious problems do not automatically mean that a couple need separate. Unlike Arthur and Tito, difficulties may have not reached the point of no return. In such a situation, poor communication is the result of underlying problems, and there's still an attempt to get through to each other. The poor communication is *not* serving to avoid the break-up talk because the couple isn't at that point—yet. For example, if you have a fundamental investment in being "right" whenever you disagree with your lover, it will be difficult if not impossible to switch to a problem-solving mode. Perhaps you need to "be right" in order to be in control, which in your mind protects both of you. As with Christian who was quoted earlier, some folks feel that that if they aren't always in charge the ship will sink. Being "right" is one way to maintain that illusion.

It is possible, by addressing this issue in therapy, to resolve your need to be in control. You can *emotionally* learn that letting go is okay and safe. You may then be able change disagreements into negotiations where problem solving becomes your focus.

Obviously, the quicker you attend to something like this, the better. There does come a point of no return as it did with Arthur and Tito. Perhaps some changes in the brain occur in which one *can no longer go back to being in love.* If you love your lover and have an investment in your future together, you'd want avoid that by taking action as soon as possible. You don't have until the fifteenth of never.

Not So Fast—Your Relationship May Not Be in Any Trouble

Before we look at some of the signs of a relationship at risk, it's imperative to avoid concluding that all problems, even significant ones, mean potential disaster. All relationships have their "not much fun" sides, and that doesn't necessarily portend major trouble. This includes the following:

- *Early problematic communication.* After the initial "madly in love" phase, you may discover that you have some problems understanding each other. That can be resolved, as long as you recognize it and do something about it soon. Talk about what's going on; go to a therapist if necessary. Just don't let it linger.
- *Stress with living under the same roof.* Disagreements over decorating, cleanliness, who does more to run the house, etc., is normal and can be handled if both of you are willing to be reasonable and set up "rules" and agreements. For example, he cleans, you cook. If he can't clean well enough, hire someone. He pays.
- *Opposing areas of interest.* You love hiking and swimming. He loves sitting on his ass to watch movies and plays. While you do need to be able to share some activities, you can't expect that both of you going to have all of the same interests. Human differences don't equal breaking up.
- *Periods of anger and isolation from each other, particularly if one or both of you are experiencing outside stress (job, family, etc.).* Scary but environmentally related as opposed to intrinsic problems between the two of you. If it continues, you should explore if it's more than just acute stress. But all couples go through periods in which one or both partners are less emotionally available. Good communication can especially help both of you navigate through those times. It's also imperative to take a frank look at what is causing the stress. If your job is taking

the life out of you, for example, you should take your job out of your life.

- *Occasional big, loud blow-out fights (not physical).* This should, by no means, define the way you handle stress and disagreements. But occasionally emotions take over and this happens.
- *Sporadic boredom.* We become bored with the ones we love. Love is not an ongoing party. You may want to work on spicing up the relationship such as trying new activities or changing your routine together. But there will be times when you're flat-out bored with each other and this shouldn't frighten you.
- *Ambivalence about being in the relationship.* These ideas go through everyone's mind now and again. We wonder at times what it would be like to be with someone else or to be single again.
- *Sexual problems.* This is common. The heat cools off as time goes by and one or both of you may be less than happy with your sex life. This is not the same, however, as chronic discontent. As indicted earlier, it's a difficult area to talk about but necessary if you want to do something about it.

Relationship Meltdown

There are definitive red flags that identify serious trouble. Probably the most telling sign is when you find yourself generally unhappy with your partner. I'm not talking about a week or even a month, but something that has been persisting and growing and is pervasive.

You may think that your awareness of your unhappiness would be obvious. Not necessarily. Coming to terms with the fact that your relationship is in a nosedive is difficult to accept. When you've invested your life and identity with someone, it's no easy feat to entertain the thought that it isn't working.

Thus, the necessity is to crack denial if it's operating. When you're alone, relaxed, unoccupied, and alert, ask yourself a few questions. Make every effort to avoid a justification of your feelings. If you're unhappy, you don't have to decide whether you have the right to be unhappy. Try also to stay away from thoughts about what will happen to your life if you break up. This is not about breaking up. It's only about getting clarity. Those questions should include the following:

- Am I unhappy with my relationship? Not just at certain times or because of specific incidents, but the way I generally feel about us.
- What has been making me unhappy? What do I want to be different?
- Have I been able to communicate this to him?
- Is he capable of hearing me?
- How long has this been going on?
- How unhappy am I? On a scale of 1 to 10 where 1 means mildly uncomfortable and 10 means miserable, where do I rate myself?
- Do I see any evidence of change? Is it getting better or worse?
- Is this situation acceptable to me to remain as is?

Aside from subjective feelings of unhappiness, many other signals may point to a meltdown. They include the following:

- Incessant bickering
- Unremitting anger and blame
- Inability to listen or to be heard
- Disrespect
- Untreated mental illness, e.g., he has real paranoia about your activities
- Feeling controlled and unfree
- Tension in his presence
- Relief when he's not around
- Dishonesty
- Distrust
- Clandestine affairs by either or both of you
- Violence
- Addictions, not only with chemicals but behavioral addictions such as sex and gambling
- Dislike of each other; feeling that you're not friends
- No longer being in love

As lengthy as this list is, it's not exhaustive, but I think you get the point. All the problems indicated cut at the fabric of a relationship. Being together is a voluntary association, existing for the purpose of making your lives together better than if you hadn't met. There will always be difficult times, certainly. But when anguish defines your relationship, there's no rationale for it to continue that way. It becomes a mockery of what it once was and ought to be.

So should you end it now? Get your stuff and go? Right? Not necessarily. But it's time to call in the cavalry.

Therapy

A great deal of what I just described is the by-product of poor communication. Not getting through to each other can cause serious misunderstandings, mounting anger, disrespect, acting out (e.g., affairs to get even) and a general sense of tension and unhappiness. For example, your partner may be terrified of intimacy and retreat at gestures of closeness. Perhaps you walk over to him while he's reading the newspaper and try to hug him. He abruptly gets up and "needs" a glass of water. You interpret that as rejection and insensitivity. You then say something provoking like "Why are you such a cold fish?" which he interprets as an uncalled-for attack. Now he's angry with you.

Months, and even years of these interactions can cause meltdown problems such as those described. The root of the difficulties is defective communication.

Couples counseling can be very helpful in improving communication and breathing new life into a failing relationship. However, a number of important points should be kept in mind. Sometimes, the situation has reached the point of no return as with Tito and Arthur. We will explore how to deal with that shortly.

Not everything is about communication, and couples counseling is not always the first or even appropriate intervention to seek. Addictions, for example, need specific treatment in their own right. If one or both of you are actively addicted, those behaviors must be brought under control prior to considering couples counseling. Addictions are not the result of faulty communication. Furthermore, learning effective communication while actively addicted is impossible.

Mental illness must also be treated independently. If either of you are severely depressed or paranoid, for example, couples counseling is not going to be effective. You can't reason with paranoid delusions or give one motivation when serious depression has sapped that. The good news is that effective treatments are available for mental illness. Once those problems are under control, you may then be able to effectively participate in couples counseling.

If you are being physically attacked, *do not seek couples counseling*. I strongly encourage you to look for, separately, a mental health professional trained in working with gay domestic violence. Going to couples counseling when there's battering can make the situation worse and even extremely dangerous. Find an expert counselor who can aid you in taking the proper course of action.

Barring these problems, couples counseling can quiet the din, clarify issues, and help both of you figure out what you want and if this is achievable. Frequently, underneath rage and discord are hurt and misunderstandings. The therapist can help you identify those issues and assist you in talking about them. If you blow up at your partner's inattention but can now say that you feel hurt when ignored, you're both in a much better position to find a solution to this dilemma.

Couples counseling can provide a safe environment in which each of you gets the opportunity to listen and be heard. The therapist can establish structure that permits only one person to speak at a time, prohibit words that trigger outbursts, teach listening skills, and bring to light nonverbal communication.

The therapist can achieve this latter point by pointing out what you are doing in the here and now. For example, if you say to your lover "Sure we can go out with your friends this weekend" with your arms crossed and a scowl on your face, the therapist can point this out to you and speak to how body language sends mixed, confusing messages to your partner.

The therapist can also give homework assignments on better communication strategies (e.g., agree to no yelling, no put downs, etc.) and then discuss results during sessions.

The therapist can help you appreciate each other's histories. Frequently, couples know relatively little about their partner's background, let alone how that background contributed to making him the man he is today. A therapist can provide the time and space for you to tell each of your stories. This can create a deeper understanding of who you both are, and why you're that way, thus helping to improve communication.

Couples Such As Tito and Arthur

In this situation, the therapist would help bring the paramount conflictual issues out in the open. He or she would help Tito talk about his desires for change, what was important for him now, and how the life changes of losing his friends affected him. Arthur would talk about his needs for stability and normalcy and that what he had now was not what he had planned for, expected, nor wanted.

Generally speaking, therapists don't *tell* you what's going on; they enable you to find out for yourself. Therapists are human (really!) and have their opinions, values, and beliefs, but they should not impose their values on their clients. I have pointed out how the relationship between Tito and Arthur is no longer viable. The therapist may see that immediately. Nevertheless, an open mind should prevail. Sometimes the unexpected happens. Perhaps hearing about Tito's experience of the loss of his friends might change something in Arthur that could affect the dynamic of the relationship. Not likely, but possible.

If, however, it remains clear that the men are going in irreconcilable directions, the therapy would focus on helping them separate in a healthy manner. This would involve mitigating blame and underscoring that differences are simply differences, not indications of right or wrong, good or bad. It's common and perhaps natural to blame one's ex for a relationship that has failed. This has serious implications for the future relationships. If you think your ex was the anti-Christ, you'll carry that thinking and bitterness into a new relationship (not to mention your life in general). To appreciate that you simply had different needs and that no one was "bad" is liberating. That would certainly be the goal with Tito and Arthur.

Therapy should also be aimed at helping them prepare for the transformation in identity (from couple to single), and strategize the necessary tasks (moving out, dividing property, etc.) to uncouple.

The Future

Perhaps you've been in a relationship that died a miserable death. Maybe you were as unhappy as Tito and Arthur. Maybe you had a relationship that could have continued had you been able to communicate. You still loved each other and wanted to be together, but that wasn't enough. Perhaps you're having difficulties with your current boyfriend.

Whatever your situation, the future can be bright. Good communication is the heart and soul of a happy relationship. And you can effectively communicate, no matter how brain dead you've been in the past, no matter what you feel right now, no matter how many of your relationships burned to the ground.

We have explored throughout this book numerous forces that impede effective communication. Whether it's entombed feelings, inappropriate anger, avoidance of "taboo" subjects, or mistaking your current boyfriend for your wicked ex, you now know the enemy intimately. That means at least half of the battle is won. You can dismantle those forces, and get through to the lover next to you, or the man you have yet to meet. You own that choice.

Chapter 10 will examine the means to enhance and protect the most important relationship you may ever have in your life.

Chapter 10

Affirmative Communication: Sharing Feelings, Love, and Life

... what's really unique and wonderful about my relationship is we're having fun every single day. We really enjoy being together . . . Just knowing that he's sitting at the other end of the table is really comforting and really wonderful.

Danny, 31, teacher
Austin, Texas

... our relationship is successful . . . I think that honesty and trust are very important and you have to work at something that you really want, no matter what it is. And I feel very fortunate that I have been able to have that . . .

Bradley, 39, police officer
New York City

It certainly allows me to change and grow in ways that I wouldn't if I didn't have somebody that was with me throughout all those years . . .

Simon, 34, attorney
Madison, Wisconsin

Being in love is an extraordinary privilege. Your bond is as unique as DNA, as are your experiences. It could be dropping ice cream on yourself precisely when he glances at you. Your eyes lock as you both laugh. It could be discovering that your best friend has suddenly died, and he's there to support you.

These experiences provide color and depth to what is a short, mysterious journey called life. They take you to places neither one of you

Man Talk: The Gay Couple's Communication Guide
© 2007 by The Haworth Press, Inc. All rights reserved.
doi:10.1300/5527_11

could have arrived at on your own. Sad, in my view, is to go through this passage without ever having been in love.

So if you're in love, or in search of a relationship, consider this: Love is a supreme gift, and you need to do everything possible to nurture and protect that offering.

Love can be lost by an act of the cosmos, and there's nothing you can do about that. But it can also vanish by an act of human choice—more often, in fact; that, you can control.

What I'm about to ask you to do works best if both you and your partner participate. But that may not be the case. Therefore, consider what I say irrespective of what he does. Of course, it's impossible to have one-sided affirmative communication. But when you change, you change the relationship system, and that will impact his behavior. If you both wait around for the other to "go first," you'll be waiting until ice cream companies do a thriving business in hell.

How You Treat Each Other

> ...then you settle into it...you become more relaxed...you don't feel that it is as important to jump in there and make sure you're part of the game...and then things can go wrong. If you don't water a plant, it's going to die.
>
> Bradley, 39, police officer
> New York City

> Then you get into the middle period, a few years into it and you really do...have to watch out for becoming stale. And taking each other for granted...the ones who don't succeed [break up] are the ones who don't ever figure out that "oh my God we're taking each other and this relationship for granted."
>
> Simon, 34, attorney
> Madison, Wisconsin

People in relationships often become sloppy as familiarity develops. As weeks become months and years, you may do things you wouldn't dream of doing when courting. You'd never say, "shut up" or "you don't know what you're talking about," on a first date. If you did, and your date was sane, you'd never see him again, yet this kind of verbal abuse can take place with someone you love, care for, and are bonded with. That makes no sense.

Respect, being valued, treated in a manner that demonstrates reverence, is Relationship 101. The good news is that you can do that starting right now. No edict dictates that you must become ugly with your partner because you've been together a long time. You don't do that with co-workers, and those relationships are far less important in the scheme of your life. You certainly don't have to do that with your lover.

Recognizing the Good Stuff

Remember when you wanted a boyfriend? Do you recall all the things you imagined would happen when you found him?

Some of it, of course was fantasy. But not all. You do have someone in your life who cares, who shares the good times and the not-so-good ones, who's there when you need him. Funny about us humans. We so easily take for granted that which becomes accessible. How many of us seriously consider how fortunate we are to have food, clean water, and a roof to sleep under? We don't, and by not doing so, we limit our experience of joy. It's the same with your lover. Once upon a time, he didn't exist; now he does. That which you once craved for is now in your life! If you can focus on that just some of the time, you'll discover a whole new way to be happy. It won't hurt his spirits either.

Expressing the Good Stuff

The media rarely reports good news. "Man helps blind, crippled lady cross the street" is not considered newsworthy. "Man shoots blind, crippled lady as she crosses the street" will be disseminated across the globe.

Analogously, many of us communicate only our complaints to our partners, the bad news. When it comes to expressing appreciation, silence prevails. Some guys will say, "Oh, he knows I feel that way . . . or he should." No, he may not know that, "shouldn't" have to know that, and even if he does, how could it hurt to tell him?

Giving him deserved credit, saying you care, declaring "I love you," are some of the simplest, easiest, and most relationship-enhancing acts you can preform. They cost nothing and go far. Your lover wants to know you feel this way, and mental telepathy is not a mode of delivering that information.

Take inventory. If you love and appreciate your partner (and if you don't, I'd wonder why you're with him), you should be expressing those feelings *many times a day.* Do you? Do you do it at all? Can you remember the last time you did?

If telling him the good stuff is a rarity, you can change that. Is he wearing a fantastic shirt today? Let him know it. Did he cook dinner for you last week? Thank him. You forgot then, but now you have remembered. Do you feel good when you hear his voice if he calls you at work? Tell him.

Many of us get caught up in the ridiculous belief that doing this is phony and silly. How can complaining and pointing out problems be honest, and saying something nice disingenuous? This makes absolutely no sense, and underscores our negativistic culture more than anything else.

Relationship Cruise Control Is Science Fiction

It's fun to muse about celestial togetherness, pure understanding, flawless resonance, unending lust, and happily ever after. Relationships in the Twilight Zone[1] may operate as such, not here on the blue globe.

When you accept the fact that you must nurture your relationship, as you must care for anything that matters in your life, you discharge fantasy from running your relationship. Fantasy is wonderful and it's the basis for much creativity, but fantasy as the guiding force in a relationship will do a poor job.

Your Behavior

Communication is not isolated to speech and nonverbal cues. All behavior is a form of communication. It means arriving or not arriving when you say you will. It's the special days you remember or don't, the way you greet him in the morning, how you groom and dress yourself, how you socialize with others in his presence. If you like to be funky at times and skip showers, how does your lover feel about this? When you flirt at a party, is he okay with this? If you're grouchy when you wake up, does he see this as par for the course or is it getting on his nerves? Find out. You don't have to reinvent yourself and you must be comfortable with who you are. But if you are aware that certain behaviors bother him, you may *want* to alter them.

---

[1]*The Twilight Zone* television series. Created by Rod Serling, 1957.

Honesty and Intimacy

> . . . saying one thing and behaving in another way just creates a level of cynicism that destroys the relationship. . . .

> Christian, 36, real estate agent
> Miami Beach, Florida

Honesty is not about morality; it's about what will bring you happiness. Telling the truth is fundamental to intimacy. Truth is the expression of authenticity. Truth dissolves walls, develops trust, and forges connection. Truth grants access; dishonesty obstructs.

The biggest lie about lying is that it's functional; it allegedly saves you and him from pain, makes things easier, and avoids unnecessary problems. It does none of that. Let's explore the following scenario:

You have just returned from a business trip where you have slept with a guy you met in a bar. It happened the night before you flew home. You had a few drinks, one thing led to another, and before you knew it you were fucking him in your hotel room.

You have an understanding with your partner that you and he will have sex only with each other. This is the first time anything like this has happened. You've been together for three years.

As you walk in the door, he's happy to see you and plants a kiss on your lips. He asks you about the trip. You tell him it was fine, the usual business crap, nothing different. You're smiling, as is he, but inside you there's no smile.

You question if you should say anything about what happened last night. You know it will upset him and destroy the nice moment you're having. It will be distressing to you because you're embarrassed and feel guilty. Maybe he'll be so angry that he'll walk out the door. You finally reason to yourself that it was a meaningless fling, you'll never see the guy again, and it would be stupid to say anything. Why create a problem, you ask your self?

Here's my take on this. You already have a problem; you violated your agreement. You'll have an additional problem if you say nothing. You're then lying (yes, omission in this situation is lying). That's building a wall, which means poisoning your intimacy.

It's beyond the point whether he'll find out another way. I would only say that what you may think is impossible (the guy lives in another state, you didn't give him your phone number) often turns out to be shockingly probable (the guy looks you up; you both run into him while on vacation; he knows a friend of your boyfriend, etc.).

But even if he would never find out, you're still debasing your intimacy because *you* know. You have a secret that involves a lie. How can you let go and feel deeply connected with him when that's staring you in the face?

Telling him the truth is scary and will be uncomfortable, but it's an act of respect for you as well as him. It means admitting that you're less than perfect and that lets him know the real you. It removes any "dark secrets" and feelings that you are living less than a straightforward life with him. It gives him the opportunity to accept or reject your fallibility. Accepting you means you both grow closer. That's what healthy relationships are about. Relationships are not about living in the illusion of perfection but rather in reality with its heartaches and rewards. Healthy relationships are about forgiveness and moving on. By not being truthful, you deny both of you the opportunity to face the crisis together and grow.

There is, of course, a risk of rejection. He could leave you. But would it be better to stay together rooted in deception? Would it be preferable to stay with a man who may bolt at the first sign of crisis? Not telling the truth will prevent you from ever knowing how he would handle this. Being straightforward also gives both of you the opportunity to solve this problem. Maybe you're unsatisfied with monogamy. If that's the case, you're going to cheat again if this issue is not addressed, thus creating an even more complex dilemma.

Honesty is the less complicated, less painful way to deal with challenging issues. It nurtures your relationship as it does your emotional well-being. All affirmative communication is predicated on honesty.

Feelings

Being at peace with feelings and having the capacity to express them to your partner is the foundation of relationship.

> It's okay to be the way you are. It's okay to open up and express. I hold that very near and dear to me. I think that's one of the key components to any healthy relationship.
>
> Bradley, 39, police officer
> New York City

Yet, as described earlier, men, and particularly gay men, have challenges with expression of feelings. Socialization is not prison, however. You can overcome the faulty education. The heart of the problem of repressing feelings is needing to be in control. You don't need that at all.

Being in love is being emotionally vulnerable; the two go together. You can't dive into a swimming pool and remain dry. You can't reach the highs of intimacy within psychological walls of armor. But here's something you can do: relax. Emotional vulnerability is not a threat to your survival. *It's not a threat at all.* You may feel that way, but your emotions are fooling you, which means you can compel yourself to let go. Big boys do cry. Men can be weak, passive, receptive, frightened, out of control, helpless, and confused. Men are human, and this is the nature of human beings.

You don't have to be in charge. You, your lover, your mother, your siblings, your co-workers, will not disintegrate if you abdicate the throne. Staying on the throne will do nothing but destroy the quality of your life and maybe your actual life. How many "indispensable" men drop dead of heart attacks? And guess what? The world goes on.

You have been fed a bunch of lies, and one way to counteract that is to remind yourself daily, if necessary, that they are lies. Go up to the mirror in the morning and tell yourself what I just said. Add you own ideas.

You should also find yourself expressing feelings and vulnerability. Getting to a softer you comes from working both on the inside and outside. If you behave *as if,* you'll get to where *it is.*

The following list of expressions should find their way into your relationship and your life. If they're not there, start using them. Obviously, you have to find the appropriate situations, and it will feel awkward and disingenuous at first. Don't say something you flat out don't mean, but be aware that your resistance can come from your fear of vulnerability. If in doubt, say it! It will help you crack the nonsensical, deadly effects of male socialization.

- I'm sorry.
- I don't know the answer.
- I screwed up.
- I was wrong.
- I'm frightened.
- Help me.

- I can't take care of you.
- You intimidate me.
- What will I do?
- I feel alone.
- I'm not in charge.
- I don't want to have all the responsibility.
- I want to cry.
- I cry at times.
- I'm not staying late at work anymore.
- No one will die if I can't be reached.
- No, you can't count on me to do this.
- I am tired and feel weak.
- I'm sad.
- I need help.
- I want someone to take care of me.
- I'm terrified.
- I don't feel strong.
- I have screwed up big time.
- I don't want to be in the house without you.
- Fighting and yelling scares me.
- I get scared when I'm away from home.
- I'm afraid to see the doctor.
- I can't pick up that heavy package. It might hurt my back.
- I can't fix that; I have no ability in that area.
- I can't swim. Could you teach me?
- I feel small.
- I missed you terribly.
- You're right; I really didn't know jack shit about what I was talking about.
- I am sorry. Please forgive me.

Death, Taxes, and Anger

Anger is inevitable. Perfect harmony exists in a perfect land. You live in Brooklyn (or wherever).

Many forces in life are both good and evil. The third rail in the New York City subway system powers the trains, but it will also kill you if you touch it. It's what you do with the force that matters.

Anger can be respectful and very productive. Saying to your partner that you're angry with him communicates that he means enough to you to induce those emotions. I loathe quoting Richard M. Nixon, but he once said, "Don't get the impression that you arouse my anger. You see, one can only be angry with those he respects."[2] He was right about that.

Sharing this feeling with your partner says you trust his ability to handle that information. Furthermore, it respects your integrity, as it does his. You are not going to sit silent while he does something that injures or bothers you. You are not going to induce him to play ten questions with passive-aggressive nonsense as he tries to figure out what's wrong. You're laying it right out on the table. You're therefore giving him a chance to see the issue clearly and to respond.

Anger Can Be Pretty

Where do we get this notion that harmony is pretty and conflict ugly? I guess it's part of the "sanitized delusion" of our culture. We don't think of Jennifer Lopez letting out a nuclear fart, but we all know that she's done that, as all humans have and do!

Let go of the notion of pretty and ugly. Harmony and disenchantment are part of life. When you try to deny something, it just comes back stronger and more menacing.

Anger Is Not Violence

Anger and violence are two very distinct phenomena. One is a feeling, the other behavior. The more you recognize anger as a normal part of your relationship, the better you minimize the chances of anger converting into violence. Violence arises not from anger, but from the inability to properly manage anger.

Listen, Don't Fix

He wants to be heard, not given *your* answer to salvation. As bright as you are, you may not know what's right for him, and even if you

---

[2]President Richard M. Nixon responding to a question by Robert C. Pirpoint of CBS at a presidential press conference on October 26, 1973. *Source:* National Archives; Nixon Presidential Material.

do, he has to find that out on his own terms. Listening, as we explored earlier, is wonderfully supportive. Telling him how to live is obnoxious.

Communication Destroyers

Communication destroyers live up to their name. They may feel "good" in the moment but not long afterward. They foster long-term unhappiness and relationship disintegration. Scream at your lover with your eyes halfway out of their sockets and you may stop him cold, but then you have also stopped dialogue.

How do you avoid communication destroyers? By doing the following:

- *Express what you want, need, are angry about, etc., as soon as you can in nonattacking ways.* Example: "I'm uncomfortable paying for dinner so often, Leo. I'd like to talk about this," not "You're a cheap fuck, Leo. I'm *always* paying for dinner. Pay for your own god-damn meal."
- *Be straightforward.* Say what you have to say in simple, clear language. Some things are difficult to say (you smell bad), but as long as you say it affectionately, you should be fine. Prevaricating can result in misunderstandings. He's your man; feel safe to say what's on your mind. You'll both survive even if you find yourselves in an awkward place. Beating around the bush is for politicians, and we know how popular they are!
- *Tackle behavior, not your lover.* It's imperative to communicate your disfavor of actions. It's a different matter to communicate that *he* is unacceptable. If his persona was really appalling to you, you wouldn't be with him. So why waste time with spewing nonsense? "Brad, it upsets me when you come home late without calling" not "Brad, you're selfish and disgusting; you don't call because you only care about yourself." The latter statement is fallacious, leaves no room for change, and incites him to attack. It's not difficult to use language that focuses on behavior; it's a matter of changing around a few words! It's the behavior that's bothering you so that's what should be addressed.
- *Take responsibility for your feelings since only you create them.* "Sandy, I feel sad and lonely when you're away so often. Could

your schedule be changed?" not "You're abandoning me again. You make me feel miserable and lonely."

- *Address one issue at a time.* "Steven, please, not another Christmas with your mother. It was horrible last year. I want to spend Christmas with just the two of us. It was your decision to do that last year. I would like it to mine this time." Very different from "I refuse to visit your mother this Christmas. I'm sick and tired of you planning all of our holidays. Remember when you insisted we go to Rome and I hated it? You're always getting your way. I hate that couch we bought. But no, we had to have this modern crap that embarrasses me whenever people come into our house. You decide everything. To be honest with you, I never wanted "our" cat. I like dogs. You made me get a cat. You're running my life and I'm tired of it. And what about the damn car we have? Remember how you insisted it had to be two doors. I hate two-door cars! So forget it. I'm not visiting your mother this Christmas or any other Christmas." Oy vey!

- *Speak in a civilized tone.* Ranting and screaming is frightening, and can escalate a volatile situation into a completely out-of-control state of affairs. Yelling produces defensiveness, embarrassment, hurt feelings, and physiological arousal, which require significant time to dissipate. You and he will feel lousy after screaming, not relieved. Speak to him as you would to anyone you respect; just keep in mind that he means more to you! I recognize that yelling is, to some degree, cultural. Nevertheless it's a communication destroyer. You can change this.

- *Don't kick your dog or the man you love.* Rotten days at work need to be left at the door or don't open it. Your relationship is your sanctuary from the horrors of the world. Why debase your sanctuary? When you attack your lover because you boss was nasty, you're hurting your lover while extending the hours of your employment. You probably don't get paid enough for all the hours you put in as is. Why increase them? If you feel you won't be able to control this, stay away from home until you calm down. Have a beer, call a friend, play some pool, go to the gym, do whatever it takes to prevent taking it out on your lover. If you don't live together avoid the phone until you calm down. Obviously, work this out in advance and let your lover know you're coming home late and/or won't be available by phone. Send him an e-mail.

- *Quit Your Job (if necessary).* Few of us today have our "father's job." When my dad came home after a day of driving a meat truck in lower Manhattan, his job was over. Oh, he complained about it, but at least no one was paging him at midnight to ask him about a missing dead cow! Along with the advent of pages, cell phones, faxes, and the Internet, an attitude has developed in America that work is an almost twenty-four-hour endeavor. The so-called job experts seem to be blind to this societal pathology as they coach folks into showing their employers (or prospective employers) that they can do "anything" so as to "stand out." I have heard advice from otherwise sane people that included coming to work early, leaving late, working on weekends, and doing anything to make oneself "indispensable." I view this as incompatible with a healthy relationship and remaining alive. I mean that. People actually do drop dead from believing in and living out nonsense like this. Of course, you want to do well at work, get ahead, and make good money. But take a close look at the price. If you are working crazy hours and are chronically miserable, it's going to be impossible for your relationship to escape this. In the previous section I advised you to stay away from home until you calm down if your job has gotten to you. In this kind of situation, you may never be able to go home! Few of us are really trapped in jobs. It's in your head. You need to put your hands over your ears or start singing loudly when the truisms start flying (the economy sucks, be happy you have a job, you have good insurance (to pay for your stroke), blah, blah, blah.) Take control of your life. You may have to make a difficult choice, make less money, and start over. But how productive or wealthy can you become in the cemetery? Again, I'm not joking. Certain jobs can kill. And they will certainly kill communication and your relationship because of the severe stress they bring about. If this is your situation, save your relationship and your health. Put aside some "fuck you money" (if you haven't already) and then write a note to your boss that includes the words "I quit."
- *Play Monopoly, not "guess why I'm pissed."* If he did something wrong, you need to tell him directly. I know it may be fun to give

him those dirty looks, but there are other ways to have fun. It's not his job to figure out what's wrong and he may not be able to. Say it, deal with it, and move on.

- *Hold on to money, not anger.* Your money can grow and make you wealthy. Your anger can grow and make you sick. There is no logical reason to live with resentment—it is universally destructive. If there are long-standing resentments with your partner, start dealing with them. You may need therapy, perhaps individual work, to get through this. But when you let go you'll be lighter and can enjoy the love you have a whole lot more.
- *Threatening to break up is no longer in your vocabulary.* Take a vow *never* to say this, no matter how angry, disappointed, confused, or fed up you feel. If you sense that those words are about to leave your lips, put your hand over your mouth. I'm not kidding. *Cease and desist.* This is the anti-Christ of gay male relationships. You should only use break-up words when that is in fact what you're doing.

Secret and Taboo

Intimacy doesn't mean merging. As good as it gets, two people do not, and should not, become one. I'm sure you've observed this: "How do you feel Mark?" Mark remains silent. Joe answers: "*We* feel just fine!"

Individuality also means that you don't share every thought and feeling with your partner. This would also threaten your independence. You were a separate person before you met him, and you will remain that way forever. Relationships that work the best strike a balance between deep sharing and retaining boundaries. You enjoy a great life together, but you still have your own lives.

When it comes to serious topics *that affect both of you,* however, opening up becomes necessary. I have identified seven of these subjects; you may have different or additional ones. Issues that affect both of you in significant ways will cause big trouble if they are not handled and handled early. Sexual dissatisfaction for example, will cause frustration, resentment, and drifting if a solution is not found that accommodates both of you. That solution can't be identified if you won't talk about it.

Even more disturbing is the issue of having forbidden topics in a relationship. Simply put, there should be none. As I've said, you don't need to share everything, *but not being able to talk about something* is an entirely different matter. That's a barrier to intimacy. It sends a powerful message that your relationship is both conditional and fragile. You can let go but only to a certain degree. You can say just so much but make sure you don't accidentally say something that crosses the line. That's makes no sense. How can you feel free to let go if suddenly you could discover that you've let go too far? And does that mean that your relationship will crack under the strain?

Unconditional freedom to talk and feeling safety in the strength of your bond is imperative to affirmative communication.

> It feels great to feel so safe in my relationship . . . to know that I can be myself completely, no matter how stupid I come off sounding, no matter how ridiculous it may be, no matter how selfish it may sound . . . I don't feel like I have to censor myself . . . it's really liberating to finally be in a relationship where I don't even have to think about what I'm saying because I know there isn't anything I could say to change how he feels about me . . .
>
> Danny, 31, teacher
> Austin, Texas

If you feel that a topic is taboo, that's a signal to start talking.

Accept Him for Who He Is

> . . . people stay in relationships with others who let them be themselves . . .
>
> Brian Wolfe, MFT
> formerly in private practice, San Francisco, CA
> (now living in New Zealand)

You and your lover are who you are. Being together will expand your perspectives, and potential for change stops only when breathing ceases. But adults do not undergo radical personality transformations. If you expect that or try to make that occur, you're going to be disappointed.

You can't know the "full him" in the first weeks and months of being together, although we often get many clues we ignore. Given enough time, and especially if you move in together, you'll discover facets of his personality that you don't love. You may even exclaim in exasperation that you don't really know him when you discover an unwelcome surprise. In a sense that is true.

You will discover many of these unwelcome surprises. Why? Because humans are complex. Consider all the habits, manner in which you do things, beliefs, opinions, interests, and preferences you have by the time you're an adult. That's the same for him, and many will be different from yours. What upsets us about this is the false belief that relationship means perfect resonance. It doesn't and it can't. If you like going to the mountains, and he's fearful of heights, go with a friend and stop worrying or feeling guilty. If he's interested in politics and you are not, there is no reason for you try to get interested. Do what you like. You have separate lives and that is exceedingly important. Nothing creates relationship death faster than denying one's separateness and independence.

Furthermore, if you're open to see what *is* there, you'll find abundance. You love and care about each other. You are there for each other, both in the good and bad times. You do spend happy times together. Maybe not all of them, but certainly some. You have a history together and hopefully a future. Perhaps you share a home, the love of an animal, the connection with each other's families. Take notice and rejoice!

Time, Relationship, and Love

Time is the most precious resource in life. In fact, it is life, and you can't replenish lost time. When you freely give of your time to be with someone, you're saying, in effect, that this person is very special to you. With friends as well as lovers, we give our time because of the immense value we place on the relationship.

If time is life, then relationship is what brings depth and color to existence. Life devoid of meaningful relationships is barren and cold. It's the experience of watching life rather than participating in it.

In my professional career working with gay men in private practice, seniors, those in hospice (among other populations), I've seen death and dying up close and way too personal. One thing I've learned from those experiences is "what it all means" in the end. It means relationships.

Despite the numerous transformations in societies throughout the ages, true love remains a constant. It exists and won't change despite what appears to be increasing dehumanization in the twenty-first century. *True love* is about caring for someone like no other. It's about showing up and being there in the wonderful and horrible times. It's about being a special part of another person's life. It's about keeping the cherished feelings alive when only one of you remains.

True love. We can make fun of it. We can be angry and bitter and deny its existence. But if you've experienced it, you know there's nothing more glorious.

We don't have all of the answers to this sacred mystery, but we do know this: communication is vital to nurturing love. Love must be nurtured or it dies.

If you've found your soul mate you're privileged. Embrace and cherish this sweet, extraordinary moment. Soon enough, way too soon enough, these will be the good old days.

Bibliography

Benson, Herbert. *Beyond the Relaxation Response: How to Harness the Healing Power of Your Personal Beliefs,* New York: Berkley Books, 1985.

Brantley, Jeffrey. *Calming Your Anxious Mind: How Mindfulness and Compassion Can Free You from Anxiety, Fear, and Panic,* Oakland, CA: New Harbinger Publications, Inc., 2003.

Davis, Martha, Fanning, Patrick, and McKay, Matthew. *Messages: The Communication Skills Book,* Oakland, CA: New Harbinger Publications, Inc., 1995.

Ehrlich, Eugene, et al. *Oxford American Dictionary,* New York: Avon Books, 1982.

Gottlieb, Miriam M. *The Angry Self: A Comprehensive Approach to Anger Management,* Phoenix, AZ: Zeig, Tucker & Co., 1999.

Kaminsky, Neil. *Affirmative Gay Relationships: Key Steps in Finding a Life Partner,* Binghamton, NY: The Haworth Press, 2003.

Kaminsky, Neil. *When It's Time to Leave Your Lover: A Guide for Gay Men,* Binghamton, NY: The Haworth Press, 1999.

McGraw, Phillip C. *Relationship Rescue: A Seven-Step Strategy for Reconnecting with Your Partner,* New York: Hyperion, 2000.

McKay, Judith, McKay, Matthew, Rogers, Peter D. *When Anger Hurts—Quieting the Storm Within,* Oakland, CA: New Harbinger Publications, Inc., 1989.

Miller, Fred L. *How to Calm Down: Three Deep Breaths to Peace of Mind,* New York: Warner Books, 2003.

Paleg, Kim, McKay, Matthew. *When Anger Hurts Your Relationship: 10 Simple Solutions for Couples Who Fight,* Oakland, CA: New Harbinger Publications Inc., 2001.

Raffaelli, Marcela, Ontai, Lenna L. Gender socialization in Latino/a families: Results from two retrospective studies. *Sex Roles: A Journal of Research,* 50 (5/6): 287-299, March 2004.

Tannen, Deborah. *That's Not What I Meant: How Conversational Style Makes or Breaks Relationships,* New York: Ballantine Books, 1987.

Index

Man Talk: The Gay Couple's Communication Guide
© 2007 by The Haworth Press, Inc. All rights reserved.
doi:10.1300/5527_13

Order a copy of this book with this form or online at:
http://www.haworthpress.com/store/product.asp?sku=5527

MAN TALK
The Gay Couple's Communication Guide

_____in hardbound at $39.95 (ISBN: 978-1-56023-569-9)

_____in softbound at $14.95 (ISBN: 978-1-56023-570-5)

184 pages plus index

Or order online and use special offer code HEC25 in the shopping cart.

COST OF BOOKS_____

☐ **BILL ME LATER:** (Bill-me option is good on US/Canada/Mexico orders only; not good to jobbers, wholesalers, or subscription agencies.)

☐ Check here if billing address is different from shipping address and attach purchase order and billing address information.

POSTAGE & HANDLING_____
*(US: $4.00 for first book & $1.50
for each additional book)*
*(Outside US: $5.00 for first book
& $2.00 for each additional book)*

Signature_____

SUBTOTAL_____

☐ **PAYMENT ENCLOSED: $**_____

IN CANADA: ADD 6% GST_____

☐ **PLEASE CHARGE TO MY CREDIT CARD.**

STATE TAX_____
*(NJ, NY, OH, MN, CA, IL, IN, PA, & SD
residents, add appropriate local sales tax)*

☐ Visa ☐ MasterCard ☐ AmEx ☐ Discover
☐ Diner's Club ☐ Eurocard ☐ JCB

Account # _____

FINAL TOTAL_____
*(If paying in Canadian funds,
convert using the current
exchange rate, UNESCO
coupons welcome)*

Exp. Date_____

Signature_____

Prices in US dollars and subject to change without notice.

NAME_____

INSTITUTION_____

ADDRESS_____

CITY_____

STATE/ZIP_____

COUNTRY_____ COUNTY (NY residents only)_____

TEL_____ FAX_____

E-MAIL_____

May we use your e-mail address for confirmations and other types of information?   ☐ Yes ☐ No
We appreciate receiving your e-mail address and fax number. Haworth would like to e-mail or fax special discount offers to you, as a preferred customer. **We will never share, rent, or exchange your e-mail address or fax number.** We regard such actions as an invasion of your privacy.

Order From Your Local Bookstore or Directly From
The Haworth Press, Inc.

10 Alice Street, Binghamton, New York 13904-1580 • USA
TELEPHONE: 1-800-HAWORTH (1-800-429-6784) / Outside US/Canada: (607) 722-5857
FAX: 1-800-895-0582 / Outside US/Canada: (607) 771-0012
E-mail to: orders@haworthpress.com

For orders outside US and Canada, you may wish to order through your local
sales representative, distributor, or bookseller.
For information, see http://haworthpress.com/distributors

(Discounts are available for individual orders in US and Canada only, not booksellers/distributors.)

PLEASE PHOTOCOPY THIS FORM FOR YOUR PERSONAL USE.
http://www.HaworthPress.com   BOF07

Dear Customer:

Please fill out & return this form to receive special deals & publishing opportunities for you! These include:
- availability of new books in your local bookstore or online
- one-time prepublication discounts
- free or heavily discounted related titles
- free samples of related Haworth Press periodicals
- publishing opportunities in our periodicals or Book Division

❏ OK! Please keep me on your regular mailing list and/or e-mailing list for new announcements!

Name _____

Address_____

_____

*E-mail address _____

*Your e-mail address will never be rented, shared, exchanged, sold, or divested. You may "opt-out" at any time.
May we use your e-mail address for confirmations and other types of information? ❏ Yes ❏ No

Special needs:
Describe below any special information you would like:
- Forthcoming professional/textbooks
- New popular books
- Publishing opportunities in academic periodicals
- Free samples of periodicals in my area(s)

Special needs/Special areas of interest:

_____

_____

_____

_____

Please contact me as soon as possible. I have a special requirement/project:

_____

_____

_____

_____

PLEASE COMPLETE THE FORM ABOVE AND MAIL TO:
Donna Barnes, Marketing Dept., The Haworth Press, Inc.
10 Alice Street, Binghamton, NY 13904–1580 USA
Tel: 1–800–429–6784 • Outside US/Canada Tel: (607) 722–5857
Fax: 1–800–895–0582 • Outside US/Canada Fax: (607) 771–0012
E-mail: orders@HaworthPress.com

GBIC07

Visit our Web site: www.HaworthPress.com